BEWARE

Deception & Delusion
in the Church

A CALL TO BIBLICAL CHRISTIANITY

Bill Rudge

LIVING TRUTH PUBLISHERS

220 North Buhl Farm Drive • Hermitage, PA 16148-1718

Beware ... Deception & Delusion in the Church

Library of Congress Catalog Card Number: 96-78378
ISBN 1-889809-00-4

Copyright © 1989, 1990 by Bill Rudge
Updated and expanded edition copyright © 1996 by Bill Rudge

Published by Living Truth Publishers
Hermitage, Pennsylvania 16148-1718

Cover Design and Illustration by David A. Sabella

Printed in the United States of America

This book is the result of many hours of research, writing, editing, proofreading, checking and rechecking of Scriptures ... and prayer and fasting. I want to thank all those staff members, volunteers, and friends who were involved in this tedious task and especially God for bringing together the talented, skilled, and capable laborers to complete it.

Table of Contents

Spiritual Immune Deficiency
Running Rampant in the Church Today

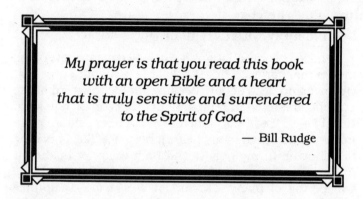

*My prayer is that you read this book
with an open Bible and a heart
that is truly sensitive and surrendered
to the Spirit of God.*

— Bill Rudge

There is a strong delusion and dangerous deception that is increasingly infiltrating the Church today. Many supposedly committed Christians are accepting counterfeit experiences and "miracles" and are involving themselves in beliefs and practices that are not only unscriptural, but also originate in the occult and Eastern mysticism.

It's understandable when non-Christians who have blinded minds (II Corinthians 4:4) and lack spiritual discernment (I Corinthians 2:14) participate in such things. But when professing Christians become involved in this deception, especially Christian leaders who should know God's Word and have discernment, it is cause for concern. Jesus showed compassion to the masses and to those enslaved in sin, but was very strong in rebuking the scribes and the Pharisees who should have had spiritual discernment.

I Have Nothing to Gain

I have nothing to gain from writing a book like this. I make no personal profit from any of my books, pamphlets, or cassettes. If I gain anything, it is increased opposition, spiritual warfare, and a possible loss of financial support. But I must be obedient to the Lord no matter what the cost!

I can identify with Jeremiah who said:

> I have become a laughingstock all day long; everyone mocks me. For each time I speak, I cry aloud; I proclaim violence and destruction, because for me the word of the Lord has resulted in reproach and derision all day long. But if I say, "I will not remember Him or speak anymore in His name," then in my heart it becomes like a burning fire shut up in my bones; and I am weary of holding it in, and I cannot endure it. For I have heard the whispering of many, "Terror on every side! Denounce him; yes, let us denounce him!" All my trusted friends, watching for my fall, say: "Perhaps he will be deceived, so that we may prevail against him and take our revenge on him." But the Lord is with me like a dread champion; therefore my persecutors will stumble and not prevail. They will be utterly ashamed, because they have failed, with an everlasting disgrace that will not be forgotten (Jeremiah 20:7-11).

Building His Church

Before becoming a Christian, I had a great interest in Eastern religion, the occult, and New Age beliefs and practices. Afterwards, I researched and exposed them for almost twenty years. Now it is sad indeed to see supposed brothers and sisters in Christ embrace beliefs and practices out of which the Lord rescued me.

The focus of my ministry is to emphasize what I stand for — Biblical Christianity — not what I am against. However, some people are so comfortable with the counterfeit that they reject the real thing. So the false must be exposed and removed if people are to understand and accept genuine Biblical Christianity.

If a foundation is laid other than Christ, we must

remove it before we can build on Christ — the true foundation of the Church. If someone began building on the foundation of Christ, but has fallen into beliefs or techniques contrary to Scripture, we must tear out the defective materials and replace them with materials of good quality.

Jeremiah 1:10 states:

> See, I have appointed you this day over the nations and over the kingdoms, to pluck up and to break down, to destroy and to overthrow, to build and to plant.

Deception in the Last Days

The main descriptive word of the last days is deception. Jesus warns about false prophets and false Christs in Matthew 24:5,11,24. In II Thessalonians 2:3,9-12, Paul cautions against "the apostasy and signs and false wonders." In I Timothy 4:1, he warns about "deceitful spirits and doctrines of demons." And in II Timothy 4:3-4, Paul reveals that there will be those who "will not endure sound doctrine; but wanting to have their ears tickled, they will accumulate for themselves teachers in accordance to their own desires; and will turn away their ears from the truth ...." In Revelation 13:13,14 and 19:20, John informs his reader that the inhabitants of the earth will be deceived because of the signs that the False Prophet performs in the presence of the Antichrist. The seduction of that deception will be so insidious in the last days, Jesus cautioned in Matthew 24:24, that if it were possible, even the elect would be deceived.

I see the elect, or those who profess to be the elect, involved in teachings, practices, and techniques of which the roots are Eastern and the occult. People are blindly accepting these false teachings that are erroneously defended by Scriptures quoted out of context. To these misguided Christians, it appears that Jesus Christ is being praised and exalted, and that benefits do result (albeit temporarily).

Today, while atheists and liberal theologians seek to

undermine the authority of Scripture and redefine the Jesus of the Bible, many so-called committed Christians are allowing "new revelations" and new teachings that go beyond the Word of God to do likewise.

Your Praise is Empty and Meaningless

You can praise and exalt the Lord all you want with your mouth and raise your hands to worship Him, but if you are involved in phenomena and practices that are New Age in nature, your praise is empty and meaningless, and you have lost your discernment.

Isaiah 29:13,14 warns:

> Then the Lord said, "Because this people draw near with their words and honor Me with their lip service, but they remove their hearts far from Me, and their reverence for Me consists of tradition learned by rote, therefore ... the wisdom of their wise men shall perish, and the discernment of their discerning men shall be concealed."

They say they are free in the Spirit, but they are in reality bound to the teachings of men. They have become clones of those who have indoctrinated them in the current trends and phenomena. This results in worship, dance, testimonies, prophecies, and experiences that are an imitation of this conditioning. Jesus, quoting the prophet Isaiah, rebuked the religious leaders by exclaiming:

> Rightly did Isaiah prophesy of you hypocrites, as it is written, "This people honors Me with their lips, but their heart is far away from Me" (Mark 7:6).

Witchcraft in the Church?

Many years ago I warned about witchcraft infiltrating churches and seducing away immature Christians. In my June 1984 newsletter, an article entitled, *Witchcraft Infiltrates Churches* revealed how several Christians had gotten involved with a woman who was involved in witchcraft and spiritualism.

The strategy of this woman, who professed to be a

born again, Spirit-filled Christian, was to infiltrate a church or ministry. She would quote extensively from Scripture, enabling her to subtly seduce immature Christians into occult philosophy and practices.

Far more subtle and harmful, however, is the fact that today many Christian leaders, obviously lacking Scriptural knowledge and discernment, and ignorant of the occult and Eastern mysticism, are now the main ones bringing it into the Church.

Why All the Deception

Before we examine some of these beliefs, practices, and techniques, here are a few reasons why deception is so rampant in the body of Christ today:

1) There is an obvious lack of consistent and intense Bible study and discernment by many Christians and Christian leaders.

2) Scripture has been twisted to portray love and unity as the highest goal of the Church. This extremism calls for unity at the cost of doctrinal purity.

3) The out-of-context and Biblically unbalanced concept of "do not judge" makes it impossible to be a Berean Christian (one who measures all things by the Scriptures).

4) There is a new and insatiable quest for more exciting spiritual experiences and "new revelations." Many are allowing subjective feelings to determine their beliefs rather than evaluating all spiritual experiences, "prophecies," and "new revelations" by the objective Word of God.

5) Many Christian leaders are unknowingly teaching beliefs and techniques that are New Age, Eastern, and occultic in nature. They have learned them at seminars, conferences, conventions, and through reading so-called "Christian" books. Yet, they still have a responsibility to test all revelations, teachings, and practices by the Word, and not merely to accept and propagate them because they are popular. If they would do this,

they would see how these teachings are plainly contrary to God's Word.

6) Others, I am convinced, who have an agenda based on New Age and occult beliefs and practices, have infiltrated the Church and are subtly seeking to indoctrinate the body of Christ.

How Far Do We Go With "Love and Unity" – "Do Not Judge"?

The Lord knows the Church needs more love and unity (John 17:22,23; Ephesians 4:13; Philippians 2:2). There is far too much backbiting, gossiping, division, and dissension. Church splits occur over the most ridiculous irrelevancies. We need to be unified in the true faith to guard against those who, in pride and lacking genuine love, take a strong stance on many non-crucial issues, causing needless harm to the body of Christ.

I will not, however, for the sake of love and unity, unite with those who propagate false doctrine that corrupts the foundation of Biblical Christianity. I will not involve myself in techniques and practices that I know to be occultic or counterfeit, thus uniting with the very spirit of antichrist.

The God of the Bible who has been so faithful to His Word in my life, and who supernaturally protected me and spared my life on numerous occasions, has not done so for me to proclaim an unscriptural message of compromise. I am compelled by His Word and Spirit to boldly and accurately proclaim His truth in love. And that is exactly what I intend to do until I go home to be with Him or until He returns.

I refuse to compromise my commitment to Christ and His Word for the sake of man-made love and unity. God will have no more part of that than He did with the Tower of Babel, which He exposed as nothing but unified rebellion.

If God is a God who advocates love and unity at all costs, as some would have us believe, then why did He stop the building of the Tower of Babel? Why did He command Israel to maintain her separation from all of the idolatry, occultism, and paganism going on around her? Why did He tell Moses to be sure His people made no covenant with the inhabitants of the land they were to possess (Exodus 34:12-16)? Why did He rebuke righteous King Jehosaphat of Judah and destroy his ships for making an alliance with wicked King Ahaziah of Israel (II Chronicles 20:35-37)? Why did Zerubbabel and Jeshua refuse to allow their enemies (even though they said, "We, like you, seek your God; and we have been sacrificing to Him") to have any part in helping them rebuild the temple but responded to them, "You have nothing in common with us" (Ezra 4:1-3)? Why did the Apostle John tell us not to receive into our house or even give a greeting to anyone who does not bring the true Gospel message (II John 7-11)? Why did God tell His people to come out of Babylon the Great so as not to participate in her sins and receive of her plagues (Revelation 18:1-4)?

The Bible speaks of a new age of love, unity, peace, and prosperity after Christ returns to this earth to rule and reign. It repeatedly warns, however, that before the true millennium on earth and the new heavens and new earth, there will be a period of unprecedented false unity on a worldwide level culminating in unified worship, political power, and economic control. This occult-empowered system of delusion and oppression is referred to as Mystery Babylon.

The current false unity movement is rapidly moving toward merging apostate Christianity and New Ageism to achieve its ultimate goals. These goals include such humanly appealing concepts as global unity, a worldwide celebration of joy, the achieving of individual godhood ("a manifestation of the sons of God"), cleansing the earth of all evil, and the establishing of "God's" kingdom.

What appears on the surface as a Christ-centered movement is in reality a man-centered movement. Revelation 13:8 gives the ultimate end of this counterfeit love and unity: "All who dwell on the earth will worship him (the Antichrist) ...."

Just Who IS Causing Division?

Many are quick to quote Romans 16:17 (out of context) about keeping away from those who cause division, but they conveniently leave out an important part of that verse. The total verse reads:

> Now I beseech you, brethren, mark them which cause divisions and offenses contrary to the doctrine which ye have learned; and avoid them (KJV).

Therefore, the ones we are to *mark* and *avoid* are not those who are causing division while standing for the truth, but we are to *mark* and *avoid* those who cause division because they are luring people away from the truth with new doctrines.

Who is causing the real divisions in the body of Christ? Not those who are standing in love and Scriptural accuracy, who rebuke and correct those in error. Rather it is those who allow this New Age, occultic, antichrist spirit to infiltrate the Church.

Paul encouraged the Philippians to:

> Stand firm in one spirit, contending as one man for the faith of the gospel without being frightened in any way by those who oppose you. This is a sign to them that they will be destroyed, but that you will be saved — and that by God (Philippians 1:27,28 - NIV).

Contend Earnestly for the Faith

In Philippians 1:16, Paul says, "... I am appointed for the defense of the gospel." Jude 3 admonishes us to "contend earnestly for the faith which was once for all delivered to the saints."

The faith that I am proclaiming today is the same faith I have been proclaiming since giving my life to Christ in 1971. I have learned, adapted, and changed a few things here and there, but my basic message of Biblical Christianity stands firm. I am teaching the same Biblical principles God taught me through His Word and Spirit many years ago. These principles have proven far superior than Eastern, occult, and New Age beliefs and techniques in enabling a person to reach their maximum potential in Christ.

No, I have not changed! These supposed brothers and sisters have changed. They have turned aside to the right or to the left (Deuteronomy 28:14; Joshua 1:7; II Kings 22:2) and forsaken their pure devotion to Christ and His Word. They have accepted new teachings, new phenomena, "new revelations," and "new truth" — which go beyond the Word of God. They have involved themselves in groups, movements, beliefs, and practices which have compromised their commitment to Biblical Christianity and brought an unholy mixture into the Church. Many of them are, in reality, now proclaiming "another Jesus, another gospel, and another spirit" — and multitudes who don't know God's Word are getting caught up in it.

Paul writes to the Galatians:

> You were running well; who hindered you from obeying the truth? This persuasion did not come from Him who calls you. A little leaven leavens the whole lump of dough (Galatians 5:7-9).

I John 2:18,19 admonishes:

> Children, it is the last hour; and just as you heard that antichrist is coming, even now many antichrists have arisen; from this we know that it is the last hour. They went out from us, but they were not really of us; for if they had been of us, they would have remained with us; but they went out, in order that it might be shown that they all are not of us.

II John 7-11 warns:

For many deceivers have gone out into the world, those who do not acknowledge Jesus Christ as coming in the flesh. This is the deceiver and the antichrist. Watch yourselves, that you might not lose what we have accomplished, but that you may receive a full reward. Anyone who goes too far and does not abide in the teaching of Christ, does not have God; the one who abides in the teaching, he has both the Father and the Son. If anyone comes to you and does not bring this teaching, do not receive him into your house, and do not give him a greeting; for the one who gives him a greeting participates in his evil deeds.

In the early days of my ministry, I rubbed shoulders with many Christian leaders, about whom I was uncertain. Their message wasn't blatantly unscriptural, but their experiences and beliefs caused me to wonder. I knew in my spirit that something was wrong; I just wasn't quite sure what it was. Then years later as I matured in Christ and the knowledge of His Word, their teachings and techniques became visibly unbiblical. I now know why I had skirmishes with these people years earlier.

Will the Real Christianity Please Stand Up?

Today we are seeing Biblical Christianity (those who are going by the faith which was once for all delivered to the saints by God's Word) being replaced by what I call "New Age Christianity." A whole new Christianity is being developed by those who are embracing New Age philosophies and revelations of so-called prophets and apostles. They think it is the outpouring of God's Spirit — revival, renewal, and restoration. It is, however, the fulfillment of Biblical prophecy concerning the apostasy and deception that Jesus, Paul, John, and Peter warned about and foretold would permeate the generation immediately preceding Christ's return.

The unity many are seeking to establish is not a unity based upon Biblical truth. It is a unity based on "signs and wonders," the experiential, and an agreement not to disagree with one another. "You don't question me or my teachings and practices, and don't call me into account with God's Word, and I won't question or call you into account."

It is amazing how those who supposedly advocate love and unity become so hostile, unloving, vengeful, and divisive when opposed, exposed, or Scripturally corrected. Some "Christians" are becoming spiritual terrorists by refusing to deal head-on with Scripture and the facts. Instead, they "run behind the back" to whisper, mutter, and undermine. They smile and act so friendly to your face, with a surface appearance of love, but their true bitterness and desire for revenge quickly manifests as they subtly or blatantly verbally stab you in the back.

Even solid evangelical leaders are distancing themselves from contenders of the faith, whom they label as contentious and divisive, but are themselves drawing closer into fellowship with groups that practice much of what we are exposing. They cannot see that unity at the expense of truth is not unity at all, but the endorsement of syncretism and false teaching. This kind of unity did not work for Israel when she tried to serve both Yahweh and Baal, and it will not work today. God was furious then with her idolatry, and He is no less angered by today's attempts at false unity.

Even more offensive are those who tolerate error so they can continue to raise funds from certain groups, be on their TV shows, and travel in their circles. They do it for monetary gain, notoriety, and influence.

Do Not Judge

While I was speaking to one of many such groups, the Lord strongly urged me to speak out against some of the false teachings they endorsed. At the conclusion I gave the following invitation to everyone: "If you have a disagreement, or if anything I have said is unscriptural, now is your opportunity to correct me publicly." But not one person said a word.

I even told the leader I would be happy to meet with any pastor or representative from her group to Scripturally evaluate these issues. Again, there was no response.

While several did respond to the altar call and repent, the leader and some of the others who refused to do so — those who are so much against "judging" and so much in favor of "love and unity" — cowardly retaliated behind my back, attempting to discredit what I had said.

When the leader was later confronted by a member of the group, who reminded her of my public challenge, the leader made an excuse that she didn't hear everything I said because for much of the time she had been "praying in the Spirit." This is also unscriptural, because Scripture teaches us to examine all things carefully. I have seen Hare Krishna devotees do something similar when I tried to share the evidence and uniqueness of Jesus Christ with them, but never a Biblical Christian. This Christian leader was wrongly using "praying in the Spirit" in the same blocking manner as the Krishnas would use their chanting.

Ironically, these leaders, who after much prayer had concluded that the Lord directed them to ask me to speak, did not feel led of the Lord to accept the message He sent me to proclaim.

When I speak to such groups, it reminds me of Stephen (Acts 7:1-60) or Paul (Acts 22:1-23) who made their defense to the Jewish leaders. As long as they were reviewing the way God dealt with the Jews in the Old Testament or conveying their salvation experience, the Jewish leaders remained civil, because they were hearing what they wanted to hear. But, when Stephen or Paul gave them words of correction from the Holy Spirit and the Scriptures, or said something that offended them, they became extremely hostile and wanted to kill them (Acts 7:51-54; 22:21-23).

So too, when I share my testimony and some of the many miracles the Lord has done, they love it and listen intently, but if I give a word of caution or warning concerning all the New Age and occult techniques and beliefs that are infiltrating the Church or their need to repent of spiritual adultery, their countenance changes.

An expression of hostility comes onto many of their faces. The atmosphere gets tense as they resist, stiffen their necks, and harden their hearts.

Allow me to point out a Scriptural distinction here. When we are dealing with a personal problem between two Christians, or someone in sin, we should attempt to deal with it privately. If he does not receive it, then take one or two witnesses and in their presence confront him again, but if that person still refuses to listen, then we are to take it publicly before the church (Matthew 18:15-17).

On the other hand, there are numerous Scriptural accounts of dealing with error and false teachings that should be dealt with publicly, since they are being openly proclaimed.

Beware of Wolves Dressed in Sheep's Clothing

To those of you who would say, "Judge not," let me remind you that every time you speak out against abortion, pornography, child molestation, homosexuality, drug abuse, Halloween, cults, and so on, you are "judging." In order to be wise and discerning, one must make sound judgments. So be consistent and not hypocritical in your treatment of this subject.

The phrase "do not judge" used in Matthew 7:1-5 is being twisted, misinterpreted, and taken out of context. As a result, it is creating a dangerous environment that discourages Biblical discernment.

Yet in this very chapter it tells us to "Beware of the false prophets, who come to you in sheep's clothing, but inwardly are ravenous wolves" (Matthew 7:15). How can I identify wolves in sheep's clothing unless I use discernment and "judge" their doctrine and fruit? How can we beware unless we evaluate and critique them in accordance with God's Word?

If a "sheep" comes into the flock and begins biting, chewing, eating, and killing the other sheep, it doesn't take much discernment to know this creature is not a sheep, but a wolf in sheep's clothing. Many false teachers conceal themselves behind the smoke screen of "do not judge," causing many believers and their shepherds to feel guilty about their God-ordained duty to discern.

Have You Been Spiritually Violated?

We are appalled at news accounts of people who sit idly by watching someone on the street being raped or murdered without intervening or getting help, yet that same mentality has infiltrated the Church. What this unbiblical attitude is really saying is: "Don't confront people when they are in error. Don't stand up for the truth. Don't Biblically evaluate teachings and practices. Don't be a Berean Christian. Don't follow the example of Jesus and Paul and other New Testament writers. Don't expose error. Don't contend earnestly for the faith. Just flow along in the spirit of love, unity, convenience, compromise, and conformity."

People are being spiritually raped today, and anyone who attempts to intervene or Scripturally deal with the issues is labeled as unloving, gossiping, judging, attacking, witch hunting, holding an inquisition, being negative, divisive, hurting the Body, being a Pharisee, being self-righteous, and the like. This mentality in the Church today is really a spirit of fear, cowardice, and compromise. As a result, shepherds stand idly by while the wolves ravage the unsuspecting flock. Woe to you false shepherds who lead God's sheep astray, for one day you will stand before God to give an account for your compromising and cowardly behavior!

Who Really Troubles the Body?

"New Age Christian" leaders imply that those who are exposing error in the Church, who are standing uncompromisingly and boldly for Biblical truth, and who are refusing to unite with their false teachings are "troubling the Body." Their attitude reminds me of King Ahab whose sin brought judgment on Israel. When he saw Elijah, he asked accusingly, "Is this you, you troubler of Israel" (I Kings 18:17)? Elijah responded:

> I have not troubled Israel, but you and your father's house have, because you have forsaken the commandments of the Lord, and you have followed the Baals (I Kings 18:18).

I will not stand by as people are being spiritually raped, just as I would not stand by if your wife or your child was being raped or molested on the street. I would risk my life to save them as I have done before on numerous occasions when I intervened to help someone.

By God's grace I will stand in integrity and commitment to the God of the Bible and intervene by boldly speaking out when I see people being spiritually raped.

Why Beware?

The motivation for writing *Beware*, the book you are now reading (first compiled in a condensed booklet version in 1989), came as a result of responding to a pastor who spiritually raped many unsuspecting people during his ministry. Initially, almost fifty of his victims came to me for help concerning occult and New Age teachings and practices he had taught them. Many more have come over the years. They were deeply hurt and confused. Several were no longer even walking with the Lord. Fortunately, however, many of them are now growing in Christ in exciting churches where genuine Biblical Christianity is being proclaimed.

In obedience to the Lord and after much prayer and fasting, I confronted this pastor alone — with restoration as my goal. Then I took two witnesses. But when he still refused to repent and would not meet with his victims to Scripturally deal with these issues, the Lord strongly impressed on my heart to write *Beware*.

Little did I know when I first wrote the booklet in 1989, that it would impact countless lives around the world. I thought I was merely dealing with a local situation, but I quickly discovered these same teachings and phenomena were affecting churches and ministries worldwide. The Lord later showed me that confronting this pastor was really the secondary issue. He was merely using that as motivation for the writing of *Beware*, which has proven to be both a warning and a great help and blessing to countless believers and leaders in the body of Christ throughout the world.

The person who motivated the writing of the *Beware* booklet tried to dig up anything to discredit me and my ministry. He even contacted my pastor and those in leadership in the movement with whom I was credentialed. When he found nothing on me, he spread lies to divert attention from the real issues. But the Lord gave me Psalm 37 (especially verses 1-13 and 32-34), where it speaks of waiting patiently and resting in Him because He will eventually bless those who trust in Him, but the wicked will wither like grass and be no more.

I know why this pastor refused to deal with these issues before the Church; he knew that the teachings and techniques he was propagating were not only impossible to defend from Scripture, but were occultic and New Age in nature. So, like a child molester or rapist attempting to conceal a double life, this pastor attempted to hide behind a facade of legitimate Christianity. Instead of repenting, he used the "new revelations" and false prophecies of so-called prophets and apostles to give him opportunity to seduce and spiritually rape many more unsuspecting victims.

When I initially wrote my *Beware* booklet in 1989, I indicated that these false teachings and unbiblical phenomena would escalate. Unfortunately, this escalation of spiritual deception has proven to be true.

Warn God's People

God is adamant throughout the Scriptures in His opposition toward those who lead His people astray. The responsibility of Christian leaders to be Scripturally sound is of the utmost importance. Their eternal destiny, and that of their flocks, depend on it.

In Deuteronomy 13, for example, God calls for the death penalty to be administered to anyone who would

lure away the people of God into following after other gods
– even if the sign or wonder they gave came to pass.
Rebellion against God's Law was punished. If God would
go to that extreme in the Old Testament, don't you think
He at least wants us today to stand up and confront and
challenge "Christian leaders" who are misguiding God's
people and enticing them into beliefs and techniques that
are New Age and occultic? We *must* warn God's people,
for they are being drawn away from pure devotion to Him.

As a teenager, I remember many guys who were so brave
and tough when they were with their friends, but were
wimps when they were alone. This is also true for many
ministers of the Gospel and Christians who are twisting and
perverting God's Word. They are so brave and bold and
confident when they are with their "support groups," but so
cowardly when alone. Although these people are publicly
proclaiming their false teachings because they are popular,
when challenged to Scripturally deal with the issues, they
are unwilling to do so. They know they can't defend their
unscriptural beliefs and involvements.

Jesus, Paul, and Others Spoke Out

Many of the books of the New Testament were written
to expose false teachings and to encourage believers to
obey and preserve sound doctrine.

Jesus, the Apostles Paul and John, and other New
Testament writers repeatedly warned the people of God to
beware of false prophets, teachers, and messiahs. They
were not afraid to publicly speak out against them using
biting rebukes and names, such as: "You brood of vipers"
(Matthew 3:7; 12:34); "hypocrites," "whitewashed tombs"
(Matthew 23:27); "dogs," "evil workers" (Philippians 3:2).
Hymenaeus and Alexander are mentioned by name:
"whom I have delivered over to Satan, so that they may be
taught not to blaspheme" (I Timothy 1:18-20). Hymenaeus
and Philetus are exposed specifically as "men whom have
gone astray from the truth" (II Timothy 2:17,18). Of
Demas it is said, "having loved this present world, [he] has
deserted me" (II Timothy 4:10); of Alexander the

coppersmith, "[he] did me much harm" (II Timothy 4:14,15); and of Diotrephes, "who loves to be first and unjustly accuses us with wicked words" (III John 9,10).

Today's wolves in sheep's clothing cry out that public debate and exposure will hurt new Christians. Apollos, however, "powerfully refuted the Jews in public, demonstrating by the Scriptures that Jesus was the Christ" (Acts 18:28). It did not hurt anyone but the deceivers, for it is written, "he helped greatly those who had believed through grace" (Acts 18:27).

The only ones who may be "hurt" are those who have built their lives on the false prophets and phenomena instead of on the Lord and His Word. Hopefully it will "hurt" them enough to drive them to their knees to seek the Lord with all their hearts, and motivate them to get into His Word to "rightly divide the Word of Truth," and walk in the genuine power of His Spirit.

Paul confronted Peter to his face (Galatians 2:11) for his compromising spirit and he did so publicly, before them all (Galatians 2:14).

In I Corinthians 5:12,13 Paul states:

> For what have I to do with judging outsiders? Do you not judge those who are within the church? But those who are outside, God judges. Remove the wicked man from among yourselves.

Paul told Timothy:

> Do not receive an accusation against an elder except on the basis of two or three witnesses. Those who continue in sin, rebuke in the presence of all, so that the rest also may be fearful of sinning (I Timothy 5:19,20).

Paul says in Galatians 6:1:

> Brethren, even if a man is caught in any trespass, you who are spiritual, restore such a one in a spirit of gentleness; each one looking to yourself, lest you too be tempted.

It's Time to Stand for the Truth

A well-known Scripture on love is I Corinthians 13. But there are more. Proverbs 3:12 says, "For whom the

Lord loves He reproves ...." I John 2:5 states, "but whoever keeps His Word, in him the love of God has truly been perfected ...." II John 6 declares, "And this is love, that we walk according to His commandments ...." And Jesus said in John 14:15, "If you love Me, you will keep My commandments."

We are living in a day and age when we must stand up not only with love, but also with courage and boldness to confront, expose, and seek to Scripturally correct error. I have had to stand alone on many occasions against cultists, occultists, New Agers, and even supposed Christians who have distorted God's Word.

Jeremiah 1:17-19 encourages:

> "Get yourself ready! Stand up and say to them whatever I command you. Do not be terrified by them, or I will terrify you before them. Today I have made you a fortified city, an iron pillar and a bronze wall to stand against the whole land — against the kings of Judah, its officials, its priests and the people of the land. They will fight against you but will not overcome you, for I am with you and will rescue you," declares the Lord (NIV).

Over the years the Lord has led me to speak out in love concerning several teachings and groups. This resulted in much temporary uproar and opposition because many were initially convinced I was totally wrong and out of line. In time, however, the Lord has always vindicated me. Sometimes it was only a matter of weeks. Other times it took years, but the Lord has always been faithful, as my track record over the years confirms.

The difficulties, opposition, and spiritual warfare incurred have been worth it. Many of those involved in these various teachings and groups have eventually called, written, or come by the ministry center to inform me that they have repented before the Lord, discontinued their involvement, and have renewed their desire to totally live for the Christ of the Bible and Biblical Christianity.

A Scriptural Perspective

People frequently ask my opinion about various pastors or churches. Although it is Scripturally justifiable, I generally try not to take a position on a person or church, or mention names. Instead, I try to take a stance on teachings and techniques after evaluating them Biblically. Then I seek to present a Scriptural perspective. That is what we are going to do throughout the rest of this book.

Are Psychospiritual Techniques Biblical? Inner Healing, Visualization, Imaging ...

Psychospiritual techniques are replacing the genuine transforming power of the Holy Spirit in many Christians' lives. Many supposed believers in Christ are accepting these counterfeit and inferior spiritual experiences instead of choosing to walk in obedience to God's Word and knowing the genuine power of His Holy Spirit.

Many don't want to hear about repentance, commitment, obedience, discipline, and self-control. These Biblical principles of spiritual growth are not quick and easy. They take time, effort, and dedication — and there is a cost.

Therefore, many look to some psychospiritual, New Age, or Eastern technique and try to Christianize it. But you can't Christianize these techniques. They are contrary to Scripture and rooted in occultism.

God's way is far superior. I have obtained greater physical, emotional, and spiritual health through applying Biblical principles than I ever did through any other means.

How Dangerous is the New Age?

In an article entitled, *Escaping the New Age,* by Paul McGuire, his answer to the question, "How dangerous is the New Age?" was:

There are two great dangers. One is New Age thinking infiltrating the Christian church through things such as relaxation exercises, visualization, imaginary Jesus's, various forms of mind control, meditation and stress management. You scc a lot of these things taught in Christian churches and much of it is occult influenced or Eastern mysticism-based .... An equal danger is an over reactionary paranoia in the Christian culture where something is called New Age when it isn't.[1]

Imagery and Visualization

What some people call imaging and visualization is nothing more than mentally picturing Biblical accounts. What some people call inner healing is merely praying for forgiveness and healing of past hurts. What some people call meditation is nothing more than concentration and focusing one's attention on the skill being learned. And what some people call hypnosis is just relaxation or reinforcing Scripture. These are for the most part harmless but unadvised uses of New Age jargon.

Imaging and visualization in the true sense is the technique of actively forming a mental picture in the mind, with the intent of changing the material world or the spiritual realm. This technique is used extensively, but not exclusively, in the inner healing ministry. For example, one is first instructed to image or visualize a scene, a situation, a person, or a confrontation, and then to imagine Jesus entering the picture, where the scene is reenacted with Jesus now healing all the particular scars incurred during that incident. One grave danger is that the Jesus imaged is not said to be an image, but the real Jesus, actually dialoguing with the person.

Johanna Michaelsen, who was deeply involved in the occult, but is now a Christian, states in her book, *Like Lambs to the Slaughter:*

There are perfectly valid and legitimate uses of the imagination .... An artist 'sees' the finished painting or sculpture in his mind or an architect 'visualizes' the building he is working on .... When we recall past events in our lives, we do so with mental images. Listening to a storyteller or reading a book can produce vivid mental images. When I studied theater, I mentally rehearsed my roles. Such envisioning is not what I'm talking about. What I'm talking about is a technique of creating an image in your mind and using that image in an *effort to create or control reality through mind-powers.*[2]

Entering the Realm of Sorcery

Many who practice guided imagery and visualization do subtle Scripture changes. For example, Romans 8:29 which speaks of "being changed into the image of Jesus," is twisted to "being changed into the Jesus we image."

While I'm all for mentally rehearsing Scripture and using imagination for Biblical accounts, I am against attempting to create spiritual reality, or to cause spiritual experiences through any mind technique. Any time you attempt with your mind to change, alter, or create reality, you are then entering the realm of sorcery.

When those who practice imagery and visualization believe that the Jesus being imaged in their minds is not just an image, but the real Jesus (even going so far as to dialogue and touch Him), then they have opened the door to counterfeit spirit guides.

You may think you are praying to the God of the Bible. Your motive might be right, but if your method is wrong, it can open you up to deception and familiar spirits.

You should never picture Jesus or God the Father in the room with you as you pray. This opens your mind to a false entity who is a product of your imagination or an evil spirit disguising itself as the Holy Spirit, Jesus, God the Father, or an angelic being.

You might think you're focusing on Jesus. You might have a real spiritual experience. But, when you create Jesus in your mind, He is not the historic Jesus of the Bible. He is YOUR experience of that Jesus. The Bible warns about "another Jesus." Many, through these techniques, have testified that the Jesus they encountered was not the resurrected Christ, but another Jesus, a counterfeit, "the angel of light" impersonating the Jesus of the Bible.

Long before it became a popular practice in Christian circles, Napoleon Hill wrote about imagery and visualization in his book, *Think and Grow Rich.* He writes:

> The THIRTEENTH principle is known as the sixth sense, through which Infinite Intelligence may and will communicate voluntarily, without any effort from, or demands by, the individual .... Step by step, through the preceding chapters, you have been led to this, the last principle. If you have mastered each of the preceding principles, you are now prepared to accept, *without being skeptical,* the stupendous claims made here ....
>
> Just before going to sleep at night, I would shut my eyes, and see, in my imagination, this group of men seated with me around my council table ....
>
> After some months of this nightly procedure, I was astounded by the discovery that these imaginary figures became apparently real.
>
> Each of these nine men developed individual characteristics, which surprised me ....
>
> These meetings became so realistic that I became fearful of their consequences, and discontinued them for several months. The experiences were so uncanny, I was afraid if I continued them I would lose sight of the fact that the meetings were purely *experiences of my imagination.*[3]

In an article in the *New Age Journal* on "The Healing Power of Imagery," a medical doctor shares many of the supposed benefits of imagery and visualization, but reveals that this New Age healing method is in reality "Old Age" occultism because you are encouraged to contact your inner advisor. He states:

> After you've gotten comfortable with your imagery, you may want to explore it further, searching for new ways to support your self-healing. You may want to

meet your inner advisor .... Whatever you believe — that the adviser is a spirit, a guardian angel, a messenger from God, a hallucination, a communication from your right brain to your left, or a symbolic representation of inner wisdom — is all right. The fact is, no one knows what it is with any certainty. We can each decide for ourselves ....

Sometimes people will encounter religious figures like Jesus, Moses, or Buddha, while others will find an angel, fairy, or leprechaun. People sometimes encounter the advisor as a light or a translucent spirit .... The best way to work with this and any other imagery experience is just to let the figures be whatever they are. Welcome the advisor that comes and get to know it as it is.[4]

You're Not Imaging the Real Jesus

A woman having problems with fear was introduced to visualization and inner healing by a friend. They started with prayer as they held hands facing each other. Then the woman was told to visualize Jesus on the cross, but all she could visualize was the bottom of the cross and his legs. She quickly realized they were not the legs of Jesus, but those of her deceased father. So she was told to visualize a past traumatic experience with her father and picture in her mind Jesus there with her.

She got to the place where she was able to visualize Jesus, but he was at a distance and she wasn't able to see his face clearly because he was wearing a hood that was attached to his robe. She was told to visualize him closer. As she did, he immediately became so close she could only see the white garments on his chest.

She then was told to wrap her arms around this Jesus. She just couldn't bring herself to do so, although that was what she really wanted. She was told to picture Jesus putting his arms around her and to feel his love. Then she felt a sensation and awareness that his arms were around her, but she still couldn't bring herself to put her arms around him. Getting frustrated and not knowing why she still couldn't put her arms around

Jesus, they ended the session.

For the following two weeks she was upset with herself and was seeking the Lord as to why she couldn't put her arms around "Jesus," until God strongly spoke to her heart, "That wasn't Jesus!" Then she knew it was demonic. She now continually thanks God for His protection in her ignorance and seeks to know the real Jesus with all her heart through His Word and Spirit.

The Dangers of Inner Healing

Inner healing refers to the healing of one's memories and hurts from the past, whether known or unknown. Inner healing involves visual reconstruction of a past traumatic experience and then visualizing Jesus supposedly entering the situation, bringing His healing, love, comfort, and forgiveness.

Although we can all agree that God wants us to walk free from hurt, bitterness, hate, and resentment, it is the *technique or method* used to obtain inner healing that we must consider. Such techniques as centering, imagery, and visualization are indeed potentially dangerous spiritually.

An individual was sent by her pastor for inner healing. The inner healers supposedly regressed the girl back to her mother's womb, and along with other lies, told her that her mother and father didn't want her. The next day the girl's eyes were swollen shut from crying. Not only can these experiences be potentially dangerous spiritually, but they can be emotionally damaging as well.

The "garbage" and "stench" of our past does not need to be dwelled on. It needs to be forgiven, crucified, and buried. Philippians 3:13,14 says:

> Brethren, I do not regard myself as having laid hold of it yet; but one thing I do: forgetting what lies behind and reaching forward to what lies ahead, I press on toward the goal for the prize of the upward call of God in Christ Jesus.

After I spoke at a Christian women's group, the president of the group told me how her "Christian" doctor, who is promoting holistic health, took her through a regression process during an inner healing session.

At first she told me it made her feel wonderful and helped her so much. As I questioned her, she informed me this supposed Christian doctor was also into yin and yang, along with Eastern and occultic philosophies and techniques.

When I told her that she had submitted her mind to an occultist and involved herself in a New Age and occult technique, she recalled that she did think it strange that during this inner healing process the first words that entered her mind were "Jesus Christ, you S.O.B!" She immediately renounced her involvement, and God gave her genuine peace and joy.

Most Christians Don't Understand Occultism

If you had come to one of the soccer games I coached and saw the referee call "hands" or "offside" or give a team a "penalty kick," you would be confused if you did not know the basic rules of soccer. But once you understand the rules of soccer, you can identify what's happening on the field.

So too, if you understand basic occultism and Eastern mysticism, you can easily identify it when you begin to see it manifest in the Church. Yet, many Christian leaders who have little or no understanding of the occult, Eastern mysticism, and the New Age movement, ignorantly accept and propagate those beliefs and techniques.

Interestingly, while many researchers, as well as former occultists and New Agers who have become committed Christians, are speaking out against these activities, many Christian leaders are endorsing them because they do not have a basic understanding of the source and origin of these techniques and beliefs.

Don Matzat, a long-time leader in the charismatic renewal, wrote a book entitled, *Inner Healing: Deliverance or Deception?* After thoroughly researching his subject,

Matzat points out four basic truths about inner healing: inner healing is not based upon Scripture, but upon the psychological theories of atheist Sigmund Freud and occultist Carl Jung; inner healing is contrary to the clear teachings of Scripture; inner healing is not based on scientific truth, but theories of the subconscious mind; visualization, an element in inner healing, has nothing whatever to do with Christianity, but is an occultic technique for reaching spirit guides.

The Deception of Centering (Meditation)

Centering, an euphemism for meditation, is the act of willfully moving oneself into a passive mental state by putting all thoughts to rest. This practice may or may not involve breathing exercises, and/or "counting down." Centering (though it may not be labeled as such) is often used in Christian circles in order to engage in visualization.

One former New Ager who is now a committed believer in Christ told me after attending a seminar, which was being held in churches throughout the country, that he thought he was back in a New Age seminar. The seminar leaders were teaching a receptive audience of Christians about centering, visualization, sensing God's "active flow" within, having "SPIRIT-TO-SPIRIT encounters," "breaking through to the other side of silence" and many other occult and New Age principles and practices.

Many involved in Eastern, occult, and New Age beliefs erroneously use Psalm 46:10 (KJV): "Be still, and know that I am God ..." to support such techniques as meditation or centering. However, Scripture study will quickly reveal that "be still" literally means to stop striving or struggling, tremble no more, because the Lord is God. In other words, He wants us to completely rest in Him, in His provision for us, and in His love for us. "Be still" does not mean to put our minds in a neutral, passive mental state.

Don't Be Fooled by Hypnosis

"The word *hypnosis* is derived from the Greek word *hypnos*, meaning sleep .... *Hypnotism* is a means of bringing on an artificial state of sleep ... more accurate[ly] a state of reduced consciousness."5

I went to research a hypnotist who was speaking on a university campus. He was supposedly one of only four in the world who could do instant hypnosis on people. There was an exciting and energetic atmosphere in the auditorium that night. Many immature and undiscerning Christians could easily walk in there and say, "Wow, this place is charged with the Spirit of God!"

As I looked around the auditorium, I recognized a Christian in the audience. When the hypnotist called for volunteers, this Christian went up, sat on the stage, and submitted his mind to a man who had just demonstrated fortune-telling, divination, telepathy, and other occult practices (although he didn't call them that).

Where was this Christian's discernment? Where was his obedience to God's Word?

The hypnotist began to tell people whom he could not hypnotize to leave the stage, and the first person he told to leave was this Christian. I believe God allowed that dismissal as his first warning and was protecting him in spite of his carelessness and foolishness. But this person didn't heed that warning, for as soon as it was all over, he ran up to wait in line to see why this great hypnotist couldn't hypnotize him.

I believe the Lord sent me as his second warning. I went up and stood beside him and attempted to warn him of the potential danger of all this. I said, "What are you doing? This is occultism." He responded, "I don't worry about that stuff, I just read my Bible." I said, "Then you better *read* your Bible and see what it has to say about all this." He walked away a little irritated, but returned to me five minutes later when he overheard this hypnotist answering questions and discussing tarot cards and other more obvious aspects of the occult. Many were fooled because this hypnotist used scientific terminology, but his feats were merely mental and natural phenomena and were a front for the occultism he was really promoting.

I received a personal interview with him after his program. He told me he considered himself a "good Christian" although he didn't believe in the Bible or that Jesus was the only way of salvation. I asked if he had ever considered the evidence for the uniqueness of Christ and the Bible, but he responded that he wasn't interested in that.

Although he wasn't open to considering that this phenomena resulted from a demonic source, he told me he didn't really understand the source of his powers. "Maybe," he said, "it is from atomic energy or something like that," but he felt it was definitely beyond latent human powers.

He said he does not believe in occultism because that is supernaturalism, but he also told me palm reading, tea leaf reading, witchcraft, and so on can be beneficial to develop one's psychic abilities.

A Deadly Mixture

A brochure I received advertising a Christian Hypnosis Counseling Center sounded good on the surface. It promised to help you lose weight, quit smoking, release stress, and the like. If you continued to read, however, you would discover their true occult overtones. The brochure stated, "Universal energy takes you into a journey as you meet your spiritual guides."

This is the deadly mixture that is poisoning many Christians — terminology that sounds scientific or Biblical causes many undiscerning believers in Christ to involve themselves in supposedly innocent techniques. They are subtly seduced away from pure devotion to Christ and His Word and are involved in imitation and counterfeit practices and experiences.

You may overcome your habit of smoking or gluttony through hypnosis, but do you know what often happens? A few days or weeks later some other problem manifests itself and another area of your life goes out of control. You keep returning to bad habits because you didn't deal with the real problem, but merely with the symptom.

God wants to get to the root cause, which is your need for discipline and self-control — which come only from obedience to His Word and the transforming work of the Holy Spirit.

Occult experts Wilson & Weldon write in their authoritative book, *Occult Shock:*

> Our reasons for distrusting the use of hypnosis involve: (1) its possible similarity to the forbidden Biblical practice of *charming;* (2) its historic origin to the occult in both the East (yoga) and West (Spiritist movement); (3) the fact that a wide variety of occult powers can be developed from hypnosis; (4) often past lives 'pop-up' during standard hypnotic regression, even when there is no expectation or searching for them; (5) cases of possession that have resulted; (6) the will must be surrendered to another person; (7) a similarity to mediumistic trance states ....[6]

Show Me in the Bible

Show me in Scripture where Jesus or Paul or anyone else used such techniques as hypnosis, visualization, imaging, or inner healing. You will not find them there. You will, however, find these techniques used in occultism.

Show me in God's Word where God's presence was attained or people had spiritual experiences through self-induced trances, visualization, imaging, or any other psychospiritual technique.

Visions or encounters with God in Scripture were not achieved through any techniques or self-induced methods, but through the divine intervention of a sovereign God (Genesis 15:1; 20:3; 31:24; I Kings 3:5; Daniel 10:1; Matthew 2:19; Acts 10:3; 16:9). That's why those who practice these techniques can't give Scriptural validation for their involvement.

There are new discoveries and inventions such as electricity and cars that Jesus and Paul didn't use. But those are "physical" discoveries. I'm talking about spiritual experiences. Jesus is God Incarnate, the light of the world who came to show us the truth. Paul wrote much of the New Testament. If there were genuine techniques to bring us spiritual experiences and reality with our Creator, then Jesus Christ or Paul would surely have taught them to us. They didn't because these are counterfeit, occultic techniques which would give us imitation and inferior spiritual experiences.

Many years ago, during my research of health and fitness, I was introduced to visualization techniques for healing. It seemed innocent enough and didn't appear to violate any Biblical principles. Besides, it was recommended in a Christian book I was reading. As I closed my eyes and relaxed I began to create a mental image of being healthy. I visualized my body being healed and totally healthy, but I knew something was wrong and felt God's Spirit saying, "I do not want you doing this." I was obedient to God's Spirit and did not continue.

Shortly after that, I saw the film, *Gods of the New Age,* which revealed the occultic and Eastern roots of this technique, and also confirmed what the Spirit was speaking to my heart. Because I had discernment and was determined to wholeheartedly follow the Lord, He protected me from something that could have jeopardized my walk with Him had I continued.

According to the *Omega Letter,* Michael Harner, a leading anthropologist (who endorses these New Age techniques), explained in his book, *The Way of the Shaman:*

> Shaman is a word that anthropologists have adopted universally for what we used to call witch-doctors, medicine men, psychics, wizards, voodoo priests and so forth. It's witchcraft in other words .... If you want to know what holistic medicine is, basically, it's simply a revival of witchcraft in the western world under new terms such as: visualization, aspects of psychotherapy, hypnotherapy, positive expressions for health and healing, positive confession, positive thinking. These all come out of witchcraft. They've been practiced all around the world and you will find them in every culture on the face of this earth associated with shamanism. And now we are accepting them in the modern world under new terms ....[7]

Always Keep Your Mind on Guard

Years ago — before I was outrightly opposed to imaging, visualization, hypnosis, and other psychospiritual techniques — I did extensive Biblical research on spiritual warfare. I learned why God tells us to keep our minds on guard and protected. Putting our minds in a passive or neutral mental state is a doorway or steppingstone to the occult and opens us up to contact with spirit guides and familiar spirits (demonic entities).

James 4:7 says, "Submit therefore to God. Resist the devil and he will flee from you." II Corinthians 10:5 states, "... we are taking every thought captive to the obedience of Christ." Romans 12:2 says, "And do not be conformed to this world, but be transformed by the renewing of your mind ...."

Our minds should be active and on guard. They should never be passive, neutral, or nonresistant. Our minds need to be filled with Scripture — submitted to and controlled by the Lord Jesus Christ. In Biblical meditation our minds are *actively* dwelling on God's Word.

The Mind is a Spiritual Battleground

The mind is a spiritual battleground where demonic activity, control, and manipulation occur. In II Corinthians 4:4, it states, "... the god of this world," referring to Satan, "has blinded the minds of the unbelieving, that they might not see the light of the gospel of the glory of Christ ...."

So if Satan, according to Revelation 13:7,8, is going to control the world, and if according to the apostle Paul in II Thessalonians 2:11,12, God is going to send a strong delusion so that those who do not love the truth will believe the lie, how will this come to pass? Through the mind.

Consider all the mind-altering and hallucinogenic drugs; consider many of the movies and cartoons; consider the yoga, meditation, hypnosis, and psychospiritual techniques; consider the hyper-worship services, religious faintings, and related phenomena that puts one in a trance-like state. Consider the mind-expansion techniques and methods to raise your consciousness level and have out-of-body experiences and achieve altered states of consciousness. These are all ways to put your mind, the spiritual battleground, in a neutral, passive, nonresistant, and receptive mental state. In this state one can easily be conditioned and programmed to be vulnerable to demonic manifestations and phenomena.

I believe the world and even many Christians are being set up for a mass brainwashing and the greatest deception mankind has ever seen — the ultimate delusion prophesied in Scripture.

Is Positive Confession the Secret to Receiving God's Blessing?

I believe in having a positive attitude. I see too many negative, pessimistic, complaining, murmuring, and defeated Christians who are controlled by worry, fear, jealousy, bitterness, revenge, and hopelessness. The internal stress of these negative and destructive emotions can make you sick and turn people off to the Gospel. Love, joy, peace, and hope are attitudes conducive to good health and to being a good witness.

During the early years of my ministry, I was asked to visit a young man who had been admitted to the hospital with stomach pains. When I arrived he was in the intensive care unit with pancreatitis. His condition went from bad to worse and it appeared there was little hope for him to even survive.

Before he was transferred to a hospital in Pittsburgh, I was able to see him several times. Although he was unable to respond, and although the nurses said he was unable to hear me, I knew his mind could comprehend what I was saying. So I shared words of encouragement and quoted Scriptures such as Philippians 4:13, "I can do all things through Him who strengthens me," in an attempt to give him hope and courage. I let him know that we would stand with him and continue to pray until he came through this crisis. I also used Scripture to convince him how important his mental attitude was at this time, and that he must not give up!

In Pittsburgh, he had a dramatic recovery. When he finally came home, he said, "Looking back, the only thing I remember about the first hospital was a young man who repeatedly entered my room. He would quote Scripture and reassure me that I could make it!"

When he finally found out who I was, he informed me that my encouraging him and giving him hope, was one of the main things that helped him recover.

Positive? ... Yes — Presumptuous? ... No!

I'm probably one of the most positive, optimistic people you will ever meet. I have attempted to build my life and ministry on such Biblical principles as determination, faith, courage, obedience, discipline, commitment, love, joy, and peace. These are very positive. I believe in having "positive" and unwavering faith as I take on challenges, face "giants," attempt to do exploits for the Lord, and believe God to do the impossible through my life and ministry!

While I do believe in these Biblical principles, I do not believe in telling God what I want with a "give me" mentality. I do not believe in usurping God's Lordship and sovereignty by trying to force or coerce or manipulate Him to respond by using the right formula or technique.

While the positive confession concept as a new Christian encouraged me to walk in faith and confidence and victory, I also began to notice a growing distortion of its truth. It got out of Biblical balance. When we begin confessing our will and desires into existence or when we teach that whatever we want, we just confess it and believe it and we have it — that is more like the occultism I abandoned and less and less like the Scripture I was studying.

I believe there is a very subtle line between standing in faith and confessing His will, and being in rebellion and attempting to control God through self-centered, self-motivated confession. We are not dealing with an impersonal energy force — like people in the occult, Eastern religions, and the New Age movement believe. We are dealing with the personal, infinite God of the Bible who is sovereign Lord over the universe.

Therefore, attempting to create or alter reality through the "power of faith" is really a form of "Christianized sorcery."

"Divine Health" in a Fallen World?

There are supposed Christians who think that they walk in divine health. But just give me five minutes with anyone who thinks or teaches this and I can easily show how utterly absurd and foolish it is by pointing out "symptoms of decay" in their own bodies. All of us manifest evidence of less-than-ideal health.

I'm in better physical shape and live a healthier life than most Christians I have met, yet I cannot be deluded to think I have achieved divine health. I realize I am in a fallen, deteriorating body. Although I have walked in excellent health, the constant "giving of my body" for the sake of the Gospel takes its toll. Paul states in II Corinthians 4:16, "Therefore we do not lose heart, but though our outer man is decaying, yet our inner man is being renewed day by day." I am waiting for this body to be transformed into a perfect resurrected body at the Lord's return (Romans 8:18-25; I Corinthians 15:35-57; Philippians 3:20,21).

"Selfianity"

In many circles Christianity has been replaced by what I call "Selfianity." "Selfianity" is people desiring only God's blessings of health, wealth, and prosperity. They want to be their own god, declare their own future, decree their own destiny, fulfill their own dreams and goals. They have done a subtle Scripture-twisting — a total reversal of what God's Word teaches in context. If you remove the facade of Biblical terminology and supposed exaltation of Christ, you will find a philosophy of self-centeredness, rebellion against the God of the Bible, and sorcery.

A sorcerer seeks to use the proper spells, incantations, formulas, and rituals to control people and circumstances, to get their desired results. Many believers in Jesus Christ are seeking to manipulate God in similar fashion through "proper" confession and various other formulas and techniques.

A woman who was having problems with her car was praying for someone to come and give her a ride. When I walked in, she was very discouraged; so, as I gave her a ride, I began to share some of the highlights concerning how God provided our "miracle van" when it was totally impossible.

She became very encouraged and excited and said, "Are you into prosperity?" I responded, "I'm into the Lord! All that matters to me is Jesus Christ. I don't serve Him for what He gives me. I serve Him because of who He is." I've learned like Paul:

> ... to be content in whatever circumstances I am [in]. I know how to get along with humble means, and I also know how to live in prosperity; in any and every circumstance I have learned the secret of being filled and going hungry, both of having abundance and suffering need. I can do all things through Him who strengthens me (Philippians 4:11-13).

Then she asked, "Well, did you confess this van into being?" I responded, "No, I got on my knees, prayed, fasted, and asked, 'Father, what is Your will? You know the future. You know which vehicle we need for our ministry. You know all things. Please show us Your will, and fulfill and perform Your will in this situation.' So He showed us His will, and it was to get this van. And then for months as the van sat unbought in the car dealer's lot, we trusted Him to provide the necessary funds. He faithfully intervened in some exciting ways to provide this *miracle van.*"

Satan Exalted Himself ...
Christ Humbly Obeyed

Satan is a liar and cheat. He deceives so many Christians into trying to live an unbiblical Christianity by getting them to assert their own wills and to therefore subtly become their own gods. They settle for techniques and involvements which are imitations and far inferior to what the Holy Spirit is able to do in their lives.

Are you believing and standing on God's Word and the leading of His Spirit, or are you confessing and praying for your will? Don't attempt to force God to fulfill what you want, then hope for His blessing.

Who made some of the most positive confessions in the Bible? — Satan. He spoke such positive statements as: "You surely shall not die! You will be like God" (Genesis 3:4,5).

Another positive confession is found in Isaiah 14. It says concerning the "king of Babylon":

> ... I will ascend to heaven; I will raise my throne above the stars of God, I will sit on the mount of assembly in the recesses of the north. I will ascend above the heights of the clouds; I will make myself like the Most High (Isaiah 14:13,14).

But God said: "Nevertheless you will be thrust down to Sheol, to the recesses of the pit" (Isaiah 14:15).

The problem with this type of positive confession is that it is *positively wrong.* In contrast, Philippians 2:5-8 states, regarding Christ:

> Have this attitude in yourselves which was also in Christ Jesus, who, although He existed in the form of God, did not regard equality with God a thing to be grasped, but emptied Himself, taking the form of a bond-servant, and being made in the likeness of men. And being found in appearance as a man, He humbled Himself by becoming obedient to the point of death, even death on a cross.

As a result of this, the outcome is the exact opposite of what happened to Satan. Philippians 2:9-11 states:

> Therefore ... God highly exalted Him, and bestowed on Him the name which is above every name, that at the name of Jesus every knee should bow ... and that every tongue should confess that Jesus Christ is Lord, to the glory of God the Father.

Stand in God's Will

My desire is not to play God, to decree my own destiny, exert my godhood, or replace His Lordship with my own. When I gave my life to Christ, I dethroned myself, and I'm not about to return to that old lifestyle.

Many Christians fall away after they go through difficult times or when God doesn't give them what they want. Why? Because they are being taught an unscriptural Christianity and are not in reality living under Christ's Lordship.

My responsibility is to do what Jesus did, to humble myself, be obedient, and seek to exalt and glorify Him. I believe in getting on my knees in prayer and fasting and seeking His Word and Spirit to find His will. Then I stand and walk in obedience to God's will.

When we operate from that Scriptural foundation, we are walking in obedience to God's Word and His Spirit and are assured of His promised provision and empowering to fulfill His purpose.

When our ministry was still very young, we lived in an apartment. As the ministry continued to grow, we looked for a house to move into so we could have our offices in the basement. Instead of opening just one door so we could conveniently walk through it, God opened two doors simultaneously so we would have to make a decision.

The one house was very large and ideal for my objectives. The other house was much smaller and not as adequate. And everyone said, "Bill, you're a child of the King. You tell God what you want and He'll give it to you." I said, "There is something wrong with that. I'm not God. I cannot foresee the future. In my limited foresight I cannot determine which will ultimately be the best decision. I don't know the end result; I don't know what God's total plan is. I walk by faith, not by sight."

Then I said, "What I'm going to do is this: instead of me telling God what to do, I'm going to get on my knees. I'm going to pray and fast and find out what His will is, and then I'll be obedient to how He leads. I'll stand and confess His will, not my own."

God spoke to my heart to move into the small house. And in obedience I did. For months I wondered why. I said, "You know I trust You Lord, but that other house was so much nicer and much more adequate." And He spoke to my heart, "Trust Me!"

Then a few months later we had 3.7 acres of prime land donated to us. The land was located behind the house we were renting and was appraised at $80,000. Shortly thereafter, the Lord strongly led us to step out in faith and build a ministry center on this property. The Lord intervened in a mighty way, enabling us to overcome many "giants" and complete a half-million-dollar project without a penny of interest being paid. If I had moved into the larger, more adequate house, I would have missed the tremendous blessing and victory God gave to us for obeying His will and not seeking our own.

Do not tell God what you want Him to do. Do not try to force God to do your will. Get on your knees and pray and fast and seek His will. Then stand in faith until He fulfills what He has led you to do.

My prayer for guidance is often something like: "Lord, give me sensitivity and discernment from your Word and Spirit, unwavering faith to believe You, and obedience to do it." And then I trust Him "... who always leads us in triumphal procession in Christ ..." (II Corinthians 2:14 - NIV).

There have been countless miracles in our ministry. People have frequently said: "That is impossible! You can't do it!" And they were right — by myself I couldn't. But a sovereign God intervened and altered what appeared to be impossible. He made them possible because we were seeking to glorify Him. We were seeking His will, not our own. We were walking in obedience to His Word and the leading of His Spirit.

First Seek the Lord — His Blessing Will Follow

I have discovered a pattern in Scripture and have witnessed it in my life and ministry repeatedly. The Lord leads me to do something, or I spend time seeking Him. He guides me with His Word and Spirit and circumstances. When I am 100% certain He is leading me to do something, then I step out in faith and obedience. More often than not just about everything imaginable goes wrong. It seems impossible and defeat seems apparent. Then the Lord intervenes in His time and way and is faithful to bring ultimate victory each time.

Our land, the ministry center, and the many other miracles and blessings God has brought about in my life, family, and ministry are not a reality because of "proper confession" but because of faith and obedience. I have not sought these things, but I have sought Him — to know and obey His will, and to make Him Lord over every aspect of my life. As a result, He has greatly honored and blessed me in ways too numerous to mention.

But I don't serve Him for prosperity. My main motivation is not just to get His blessing. For if He removes His hand of blessing (which He has occasionally done) I will still serve Him.

The Lord has also greatly blessed me financially, but I have chosen to give most of it away and live a moderate lifestyle. I could easily be justified in having a salary two or three times more than I do, but I have chosen to use that money to spread the Gospel throughout the world.

Some people spend so much of their time and energy trying to get God to give them wealth and prosperity. Scripture repeatedly indicates that spiritual riches are far more important than material wealth. Jesus said:

> Do not lay up for yourselves treasures upon earth, where moth and rust destroy, and where thieves break in and steal. But lay up for yourselves treasures in heaven ... (Matthew 6:19-21).

In Ephesians 2:6,7, Paul speaks of the "surpassing riches" of God's grace which we find in the "heavenly places." In Colossians 3:1-3, he admonishes us to set our "minds on the things above, not on the things that are on earth." We are commanded in I Timothy to "be rich in good deeds," which will "lay up treasure" for us in the "coming age" (6:18,19 NIV).

The true heroes of the faith gave up the pleasures of this world to focus on eternal riches and blessings. (See Hebrews 11:8-10 concerning Abraham.)

Keep Scripture in Context

You cannot take Scriptural passages out of context and expect to build sound theology on them. Approach them in their proper context to get God's balanced view of His Word. The Bible indicates that Scripture interprets Scripture. Part of a truth might be found in the book of John and an additional insight in James or Hebrews. Scripture must be treated as a whole.

John 14:14 says, "If you ask Me anything in My name, I will do it." Many Christians today quote this Scripture out of context, and leave us with the erroneous conclusion that whatever we ask of God He is obligated to do. But look at the very next verse. John 14:15 gives you the Biblical balance, "If you love Me, you will keep My commandments." Beware that you do not become presumptuous of God's grace and mercy and forget the requirements and responsibilities that are inherent in your position as a saint of God, one who is called out and set apart for God's service and glory.

I believe the main Scriptural criterion for receiving God's blessing is obedience and faithfulness to the Lord. Deuteronomy 30:8 says: "And you shall again obey the Lord, and observe all His commandments which I command you today." And He does what Deuteronomy 30:9 says, "Then the Lord your God will prosper you abundantly ...."

Deuteronomy chapters 28 to 30 reveal that obedience results in receiving God's blessing, while those who are disobedient will be cursed by God (no matter what they confess).

Don't be fooled. Material wealth is not necessarily the outcome of God's blessing. After all, some of the most righteous people in all of history suffered great persecution and lived in poverty. Their wealth was not in material things but in the rich relationship they had with their heavenly Father and the people of God. True faith in Christ, though it entails simply believing in the one true God and in the completed work of His Son Jesus Christ on the cross, nevertheless always produces righteous behavior as a result. People who claim the name of Christ, but use gimmicks and techniques that only assert their own desires, may appear to have temporal blessings, but in the end, like grass and flowers, they will soon fade away.

Leviticus chapter 26 is also about being blessed because of obedience and being cursed because of disobedience. In fact, the only "confession" we see in this chapter dealing with God's blessings and curses is in verse 40, and it is in regard to "confessing their iniquity."

Principles on Prayer

As I sought the Lord concerning a prayer request, He impressed on my heart several Scriptural truths and principles that should all be working simultaneously. The following are a few highlights:

1) **Right Motives:**

James 4:3 –

> You ask and do not receive, because you ask with wrong motives, so that you may spend it on your pleasures.

2) **According to His Will:**

I John 5:14 –

> And this is the confidence which we have before Him, that, if we ask anything according to His will, He hears us.

3) **Persistence:**

Luke 11:5-10 –

> And He said to them, "Suppose one of you shall have a friend, and shall go to him at midnight, and say to him, 'Friend, lend me three loaves; for a friend of mine has come to me from a journey, and I have nothing to set before him;' and from inside he shall answer and say, 'Do not bother me; the door has already been shut and my children and I are in bed; I cannot get up and give you

anything.' I tell you, even though he will not get up and give him anything because he is his friend, yet because of his persistence he will get up and give him as much as he needs. And I say to you, ask, and it shall be given to you; seek, and you shall find; knock, and it shall be opened to you. For everyone who asks, receives; and he who seeks, finds; and to him who knocks, it shall be opened."

4) Do Not Doubt:

James 1:6,7 –

But let him ask in faith without any doubting, for the one who doubts is like the surf of the sea driven and tossed by the wind. For let not that man expect that he will receive anything from the Lord.

Hebrews 11:1,6 –

Now faith is the assurance of things hoped for, the conviction of things not seen. And without faith it is impossible to please Him, for he who comes to God must believe that He is, and that He is a rewarder of those who seek Him.

5) Mountain-Moving Faith:

Mark 9:23 –

And Jesus said to him, "If you can! All things are possible to him who believes."

Mark 11:23 –

Truly I say to you, whoever says to this mountain, "Be taken up and cast into the sea," and does not doubt in his heart, but believes that what he says is going to happen, it shall be granted him.

6) Do Not Be Anxious / Be Thankful:

Philippians 4:6,7 –

Be anxious for nothing, but in everything by prayer and supplication with thanksgiving let your requests be made known to God. And the peace of God, which surpasses all comprehension, shall guard your hearts and your minds in Christ Jesus.

Colossians 4:2 –

Devote yourselves to prayer, keeping alert in it with an attitude of thanksgiving.

7) Obedience:

John 14:14,15 –

If you ask Me anything in My name, I will do it. If you love Me, you will keep My commandments.

John 15:7 –

If you abide in Me, and My words abide in you, ask whatever you wish, and it shall be done for you.

I John 3:21-24 –

Beloved, if our heart does not condemn us, we have confidence before God; and whatever we ask we receive from Him, because we keep His commandments and do the things that are pleasing in His sight. And this is His commandment, that we believe in the name of His Son Jesus Christ, and love one another, just as He commanded us. And the one who keeps His commandments abides in Him, and He in him. And we know by this that He abides in us, by the Spirit whom He has given us.

8) Clean Heart Before God:

II Chronicles 6:36-39 –

When they sin against Thee (for there is no man who does not sin) and Thou art angry with them and dost deliver them to an enemy, so that they take them away captive to a land far off or near, if they take thought in the land where they are taken captive, and repent and make supplication to Thee in the land of their captivity, saying, "We have sinned, we have committed iniquity, and have acted wickedly;" if they return to Thee with all their heart and with all their soul in the land of their captivity, where they have been taken captive, and pray toward their land which Thou hast given to their fathers, and the city which Thou hast chosen, and toward the house which I have built for Thy name, then hear from heaven, from Thy dwelling place, their prayer and supplications, and maintain their cause, and forgive Thy people who have sinned against Thee.

II Chronicles 7:14 –

[If] My people who are called by My name humble themselves and pray, and seek My face and turn from their wicked ways, then I will hear from heaven, will forgive their sin, and will heal their land.

Psalm 66:18 –

If I regard wickedness in my heart, The Lord will not hear.

Isaiah 1:15-17 –

So when you spread out your hands in prayer, I will hide My eyes from you, yes, even though you multiply prayers, I will not listen. Your hands are covered with blood. Wash yourselves, make yourselves clean; remove the evil of your deeds from My sight. Cease to do evil, learn to do good; seek justice, reprove the ruthless; defend the orphan, plead for the widow.

James 5:16-18 –

Therefore, confess your sins to one another, and pray for one another, so that you may be healed. The effective prayer of a righteous man can accomplish much. Elijah was a man with a nature like ours, and he prayed earnestly that it might not rain; and it did not rain on the earth for three years and six months. And he prayed again, and the sky poured rain, and the earth produced its fruit.

9) Delight Yourself in the Lord:

Psalm 37:4 –

Delight yourself in the Lord; and He will give you the desires of your heart.

Matthew 6:33 –

But seek first His kingdom and His righteousness; and all these things shall be added to you.

The Lord has taught me that I cannot force or manipulate Him to give me my desires. But if I merely delight myself in Him, seek His will, and walk in obedience to it, He will grant the desires of my heart because they will be conformed to His own. He will bless abundantly beyond my greatest expectations.

Is Much of Today's "Prophesying" in Reality "Christianized Fortune-Telling"?

There are two *extreme* positions concerning prophecy: 1) To "despise" prophetic utterance and thereby "quench" the Spirit; and 2) To encourage or tolerate a form of prophecy that is unscriptural.

I believe that prophecy is for today. I believe the New Testament indicates that the gift of prophecy should be in operation in the Church (I Corinthians 12; I Corinthians 14; Ephesians 4:11; I Thessalonians 5:20,21; I Timothy 4:14). In I Corinthians 14:39, Paul actually encourages believers to "... desire earnestly to prophesy ...." But I do not believe in endorsing the tremendous misuse and abuse of this gift today. I will not tolerate those who speak from their own inspiration nor the demonic counterfeits which are being enthusiastically received in many Christian circles.

The *Expository Dictionary of Bible Words* states:

> The basic word for 'prophet' in the OT is *nabi,* which means 'spokesman' or 'speaker.' Essentially a prophet is a person authorized to speak for another, as Moses (Exodus 7:1-2; Numbers 12:1-8) and the OT prophets were authorized to speak for God ....
>
> The Greek word *prophetes* (prophet) is the only

word the NT uses to translate the Hebrew *nabi.* Related NT words are *propheteuo* ('to prophesy'), *prophetis* ('prophetess'), and *propheteia* ('prophetic saying, gift, or activity').[8]

Two Types of False Prophets

There are two main types of false prophets in the Bible. First, there are those who speak and prophesy in the name of other gods such as Baal (Jeremiah 2:8; 23:13; 32:32-35). This type of false prophet is very easy to distinguish, but it gets more difficult and confusing when we deal with the second type of false prophets.

There are false prophets who claim to prophesy in the name of the Lord; yet, they are proclaiming the word which the Lord has not told them to proclaim. A few examples follow:

Jeremiah 14:14:

> Then the Lord said to me, "The prophets are prophesying falsehood in My name. I have neither sent them nor commanded them nor spoken to them; they are prophesying to you a false vision, divination, futility and the deception of their own minds."

Jeremiah 23:16,21,22,30-32:

> Thus says the Lord of hosts, "Do not listen to the words of the prophets who are prophesying to you. They are leading you into futility; they speak a vision of their own imagination, not from the mouth of the Lord. I did not send these prophets, but they ran. I did not speak to them, but they prophesied. But if they had stood in My council, then they would have announced My words to My people, and would have turned them back from their evil way and from the evil of their deeds. Therefore behold, I am against the prophets," declares the Lord, "who steal My words from each other. Behold, I am against the prophets," declares the Lord, "who use their tongues and declare, 'The Lord declares.' Behold, I am against those who have prophesied false dreams," declares the Lord, "and related them, and led My people astray by their falsehoods and reckless boasting; yet I did not send them or command them, nor do they furnish this

people the slightest benefit," declares the Lord.

Ezekiel 13:2,3,6,8:

... say to those who prophesy from their own inspiration, "Listen to the word of the Lord! Thus says the Lord God, 'Woe to the foolish prophets who are following their own spirit and have seen nothing. They see falsehood and lying divination who are saying, "The Lord declares," when the Lord has not sent them; yet they hope for the fulfillment of their word. Therefore, thus says the Lord God, 'Because you have spoken falsehood and seen a lie, therefore behold, I am against you,' declares the Lord God."

Matthew 7:22,23:

Many will say to Me on that day, "Lord, Lord, did we not prophesy in Your name ...." And then I will declare to them, "I never knew you; Depart from Me, you who practice lawlessness."

I John 4:1:

Beloved, do not believe every spirit, but test the spirits to see whether they are from God; because many false prophets have gone out into the world.

Not All Who Say, "Thus Saith the Lord," Are Speaking the Word of the Lord

When I was a new Christian, I learned this lesson very well — that not everyone who says, "Thus saith the Lord," is really speaking the word of the Lord.

God had spoken to my heart and my wife Karen's heart, to go to Bible college. After a three-week mini-mission to Mexico, we were preparing to move to Mt. Vernon, Ohio, the location of the Bible college. A woman, who was a so-called prophetess and did not know what the Lord had already clearly spoken to Karen and me, prophesied over us during a service, saying we were to go back to Mexico.

I said, "I'm still a relatively new Christian and I am not that mature in the Lord. I don't know the Word very well yet, but I do know that if God told me to go to Bible college, if God told me to buy a mobile home, if God enabled us to find the very last mobile home lot on which we could put our mobile home in the city where we were to move, then God wants me there. And that's where I'm going!"

I had to decide: Do I follow the voice of someone telling me God's will for my life, or do I follow God's Word and what His Spirit has led me to do? I chose to follow the Lord, and many times since, I have reflected back on how disastrous my life and ministry would have been had I not followed His direction during that crucial decision in my life. But because I obeyed God's voice, He has produced tremendous fruit through our ministry, done the impossible through our lives, and honored and blessed us greatly! This woman, who people exalted and almost deified, eventually fell away from the Lord.

In a tragic story in I Kings 13, we see that the word of the Lord came to a man of God and told him what he was to do. In obedience he began to follow the word of the Lord, but when a false prophet told him something contrary to what God had already told him to do, he obeyed that prophet. As a result of obeying the deceiving prophet, and thereby disobeying the Lord, he was killed by a lion that very day.

The message is crystal clear: When God speaks to you, obey! If what God says contradicts what a prophet says, then you follow the word of the Lord and do not follow that prophet.

God wants you to obey His voice and His Word. Develop that relationship with Him, and do not give responsibility to any supposed prophet or anyone who prophesies over you. It's between you and the Lord. (For background information and context read I Kings 11:43 through 12:33, as well as all of I Kings 13.)

False Leaders Use Control and Manipulation

It is both dangerous and diabolical that some use "Thus saith the Lord" to control and manipulate people. One of many illustrations I could cite concerns a young man who called me because he was very confused about the teaching he was receiving in church from his pastor.

He wanted to leave this church, but his pastor said: "Thus saith the Lord, if you leave, one of your children will die." Needless to say, he was terrorized and afraid to leave.

Think about some of the prophecies today in light of what Peter said:

> But false prophets also arose among the people, just as there will also be false teachers among you, who will secretly introduce destructive heresies, even denying the Master who bought them, bringing swift destruction upon themselves. And many will follow their sensuality, and because of them the way of the truth will be maligned; and in their greed they will exploit you with false words ... (II Peter 2:1-3).

"Tell Me God's Will for My Life"

When I was a new Christian, people tried to tell me what the Lord wanted me to do. As I matured in the Lord, they wanted me to tell them God's will for their lives. I won't have any part of either one. I'll share the Word and what the Holy Spirit impresses on my heart and agree in prayer, but the final responsibility concerning God's direction for one's life lies between God and that individual.

I remember when I was a brand-new Christian, I went to a man of God whom I greatly respected. I said, "You're so close to the Lord, He speaks to you so much. Would you pray and tell me what God wants me to do?" It was a cop out. I wanted a quick, easy, convenient way to get God's guidance. He said, "Bill, it's your responsibility to seek God's will for your life. You had better learn right now to discipline yourself to get into God's Word and get on your knees to seek God's will and know His voice." And although I was at first disappointed, he taught me a very crucial Biblical principle.

In John 10:27, Jesus said, "My sheep hear My voice, and I know them, and they follow Me." We need to hear and know Jesus' voice.

If we are not on speaking terms with the Lord — so that He has to speak to someone else to tell us what to do — then we'd better repent. We'd better discipline ourselves before the Lord and get into His Word and seek Him through prayer and fasting (as the true prophets in the Bible did) so we too can hear His voice.

The Supernatural and Spectacular Are Not the Usual

Many think those who are seemingly having frequent audible voices, visions, personal prophecies, revelations, and words from the Lord are super spiritual. But I wonder where their hearts are before the Lord. Are they hardhearted and insensitive to His Spirit? Are they undisciplined to read His Word and to pray? Is the use of the spectacular the only way He can get them to hear His voice and obey?

I would rather be so sensitive and surrendered to the Lord that He can speak to my heart through His Word and Spirit — without always having to do something phenomenal to get my attention, or without having to send some prophet to get my life in order or to tell me what to do. Only in the case of hardheartedness, such as Baalam when God spoke through a donkey, or for special situations like Moses at the burning bush when He called him to lead the children of Israel out of Egyptian bondage, or when God gave Peter a vision to do something "unthinkable" (taking the Gospel to the Gentiles), did God resort to supernatural, spectacular ways of revealing His will.

Prophets Are Not Our "Guides"

Donald Gee writes in his book, *Concerning Spiritual Gifts:*

> There are no indications in the New Testament that it is the function of prophets in the church to be her guides in the sense that they guided Israel of old — by a system of 'inquiring of the Lord.' There are indeed instances such as the prophecy of Agabus concerning the forthcoming famine (Acts 11:28), or the fate of Paul at Jerusalem (Acts 21:11), where the prophet plainly

foretells what may happen. But it is significant that he offers no guidance; it is left to the individual members of the church to determine ... (Acts 11:29) what they would do, and to Paul to decide his own course of action (Acts 21:13).

Still more significant is the fact that there is no attempt to use the gift of prophecy or the office of prophet in the great dispute that arose about circumcision in Acts 15; or in Paul's obvious personal dilemma as to the next step for his ministry in Acts 16:6-10, though on both occasions Silas, a recognized 'prophet' (15:32), was on the spot.

It can truthfully be affirmed that there is not one single instance of the gift of prophecy being deliberately resorted to for guidance in the New Testament.[9]

Even though there are prophets and prophecy in the New Testament, these are not the same as they are in the Old Testament. In the Old Testament the prophet was often like Moses or Samuel who was the recognized spokesman, not only for God to the people, but for the people to the Lord. He was the mediator. In the New Testament, when Jesus died on the cross, the curtain in the temple — separating the Holy Place from the Holy of Holies — was torn in two from top to bottom (Matthew 27:51). Through Christ, our Mediator, we now have direct access to the presence of God.

There is also another aspect in the New Testament to consider — Pentecost. Now all believers can be filled with God's Spirit and be personally led by the Spirit of God. We have the promise of Romans 8:14, "For all who are being led by the Spirit of God, these are sons of God."

Bonds and Afflictions Await Paul

The account of the prophecy by Agabus, that Paul would be bound in Jerusalem, is often inaccurately used to validate guidance through personal prophecy. Looking at this account in Scriptural context reveals a different conclusion.

First, we discover that before Agabus prophesied, Paul already knew from the Holy Spirit that bonds and afflictions awaited him. Acts 20:22,23 says:

> And now, behold, bound in spirit, I am on my way to Jerusalem, not knowing what will happen to me there, except that the Holy Spirit solemnly testifies to me in every city, saying that bonds and afflictions await me.

Acts 21:4 repeats this:

> And after looking up the disciples, we stayed there seven days; and they kept telling Paul through the Spirit not to set foot in Jerusalem.

Then in Acts 21:10-14, Agabus confirms:

> And as we were staying there for some days, a certain prophet named Agabus came down from Judea. And coming to us, he took Paul's belt and bound his own feet and hands, and said, "This is what the Holy Spirit says: 'In this way the Jews at Jerusalem will bind the man who owns this belt and deliver him into the hands of the Gentiles.' " And when we had heard this, we as well as the local residents began begging him not to go up to Jerusalem. Then Paul answered, "What are you doing, weeping and breaking my heart? For I am ready not only to be bound, but even to die at Jerusalem for the name of the Lord Jesus." And since he would not be persuaded, we fell silent, remarking, "The will of the Lord be done!"

The prophet Agabus merely told Paul what was going to happen. It was Paul's responsibility to determine what he would do. We need to keep that Scriptural balance in mind.

After Paul spoke to the Sanhedrin in Jerusalem, the Lord once again confirmed that it was His leading for Paul to go to Jerusalem, for He said to Paul in Acts 23:11, "... as you have solemnly witnessed to My cause at Jerusalem, so you must witness at Rome also."

Prophets and Personal Prophecy Book

The owner of a Christian bookstore asked me to review a leading book on the topic of prophets and personal prophecy. I gave it to our Research Director, and after only twenty minutes of checking, he said it was heresy. Next, I gave it to a Biblical apologist who said it was unscriptural. Then I gave it to an Assembly of God pastor who is very knowledgeable of Scripture, and he said the foundation principles of it were built on sand. Finally, I read it myself and confirmed the book was in error.

My basic conclusion after reading this book is that the author has deviated from the truth in three ways:

1) He has taken the Scriptural promises and blessings that are for those who have faith and obedience in the Lord and His Word and reinterpreted them to be for those who have faith and obedience in prophets and personal prophecy. A very subtle transition occurs much in the same way Satan subtly changed God's Word as he tempted people in Scripture.

2) He has reinterpreted and taken out of Scriptural context almost every Scripture that refers directly or indirectly to prophets and personal prophecy, trying to justify his emphasis on multitudes of personal prophecies.

3) He is teaching "Christian fortune-telling" rather than the Biblical operation of prophecy.

Scripture-twisting

Many people who profess to love the Lord are caught up in this twisting of Scripture. Christian leaders and those who claim to be prophets use this book (and similar books) as their source for prophetic guidelines. I wonder where their discernment is, and if they really have the Holy Spirit, why does He not speak to their hearts? I wonder, if they know God's Word, why they do not see how Scripture is being twisted.

Over and over as I read or listened to materials by those endorsing personal prophecy, the Scriptures were taken out of context, the meanings were twisted, and the Scripture references given were often totally unrelated to the unscriptural conclusions they made. It was the same Scripture-twisting tactics used by many cults to lure those with little Bible knowledge and who lack the time or motivation to search Scripture, to blindly follow their beliefs and practices.

Control and Manipulation

Leaders of the discipleship movement supposedly repented of the "wrong and injurious" extremes and the "unhealthy submission resulting in perverse and unbiblical obedience to human leaders."[10] But something very similar and even more sinister is occurring through many supposed prophets and personal prophecies.

A woman from Florida, a charismatic believer who is constantly in the Word, went to a church affiliated with the prophets. She said as soon as she walked in, she knew in her spirit something was wrong. Not only did they give an incorrect prophecy concerning her, but also she said, "The people were controlled by the prophets and prophetesses in the church."

It was the spirit of shepherding and discipleship manifest through the so-called prophets. It was the same control and manipulation, the same replacing of the Holy Spirit and Christ's Lordship with a human being whom we look to for decisions and guidance.

How accurate Jeremiah was for today when he said:

An appalling and horrible thing has happened in the land: the prophets prophesy falsely, and the priests rule on their own authority; and My people love it so ... (Jeremiah 5:30,31)!

It is interesting that many of these so-called prophets only seem to prophesy flattery and great things for their associates. However, they often resort to a form of "black witchcraft" by mainly prophesying doom and destruction against those who oppose them.

I wondered why a so-called prophet of God did not detect and rebuke the spirit of deceit and occultism in a church where he frequently spoke. Instead, he prophesied blessing and that everything was right on course before the Lord.

I soon discovered he spoke from his own inspiration,

and he always had such positive words of blessing and prosperity because this church was supporting him financially. It reminds me of Micah 3:11 which says, "... her prophets divine for money ...."

Nehemiah 6:10 -14 records:

> And when I entered the house of Shemaiah ... he said, "Let us meet together in the house of God, within the temple, and let us close the doors of the temple, for they are coming to kill you, and they are coming to kill you at night." But I said, "Should a man like me flee? And could one such as I go into the temple to save his life? I will not go in." Then I perceived that surely God had not sent him, but he uttered his prophecy against me because Tobiah and Sanballat had hired him. He was hired for this reason, that I might become frightened and act accordingly and sin, so that they might have an evil report in order that they could reproach me. Remember, O my God, Tobiah and Sanballat according to these works of theirs, and also Noadiah the prophetess and the rest of the prophets who were trying to frighten me.

Demonically Inspired Prophecy

Shortly after confronting the pastor who motivated the writing of my initial *Beware* booklet, a prophecy for my immediate destruction was given at a pastors' conference he attended in 1989.

This demonically inspired prophecy sounded so accurate. It deceived many of the pastors in attendance to be persuaded that I was wrong. It seemed so close to the truth — but in reality was so far away. If only those pastors had genuine discernment and went by the Word, they would not have been deceived. But they trusted in a false prophecy, which proved to be a steppingstone into even more distorted and perverted false teachings and practices.

The prophecy of my imminent destruction proved to be totally wrong — in fact the Lord protected me in numerous, extremely dangerous situations during overseas missionary outreaches, and empowered and anointed me as my ministry continued to grow internationally. The pastors vehemently opposing me were the ones who soon suffered loss.

We read in Exodus 10:28,29:

> Then Pharaoh said to him [Moses], "Get away from me! Beware, do not see my face again, for in the day you see my face you shall die!" And Moses said, "You are right; I shall never see your face again!"

But it did not happen the way Pharaoh expected. It didn't happen the way Haman anticipated either. Esther 9:24,25 states:

> For Haman ... the adversary of all the Jews, had schemed against the Jews to destroy them .... But when it came to the king's attention, he commanded by letter that his wicked scheme which he had devised against the Jews, should return on his own head, and that he and his sons should be hanged on the gallows" (which Haman himself had prepared for the Jews).

I Kings 22:20-23 says:

> And the Lord said, "Who will entice Ahab to go up and fall at Ramoth-gilead?" And one said this while another said that. Then a spirit came forward and stood before the Lord and said, "I will entice him." And the Lord said to him, "How?" And he said, "I will go out and be a deceiving spirit in the mouth of all his prophets." Then He said, "You are to entice him and also prevail. Go and do so." Now therefore, behold, the Lord has put a deceiving spirit in the mouth of all these your prophets; and the Lord has proclaimed disaster against you.

In the same way as the preceding Scripture, the Lord showed me that He allowed that false prophecy so that those pastors would have a false assurance and security and boldly align themselves with this other pastor, thus exposing their true beliefs and eventually causing their own words to bring God's judgment on themselves.

Reflecting back on how his brothers sold him as a slave into Egypt and the Lord turned it around for good, Joseph said to his brothers, "You meant evil against me, but God meant it for good" (Genesis 50:20).

Who Would You Believe?

The opposition and prophecies about my destruction came from people who were supposed prophets and apostles who:

- had foundational beliefs about prophecy which are built on error and Scripture-twisting;
- made unscriptural excuses for not being 100% accurate;
- propagated other unbiblical teachings and practices.

Should I have believed them? Or should I believe the Word of God and the Spirit of God? In over nineteen years of ministry, the Lord has fulfilled 100% of what I have publicly proclaimed that He has led me to do, much of which seemed totally impossible to ever be fulfilled. But God has been faithful — and the end result has always been ultimate victory!

I think the spirit from which these supposed prophets prophesy is evident. It's the same spirit I have encountered over the years in dealing with many occultists. It's the same spirit that motivated someone from one of their churches to actually team up with a leading occultist and attempt to destroy our ministry. It's the same spirit that during this time spoke as a demon in a woman's dream telling her to destroy our ministry and telling her husband (in her dream) to kill me.

I may one day die for Christ, but the Lord has assured me that my life will not be taken until His purpose is fulfilled. My prayer is: "Lord, let me have the grace, the power, the boldness, and the forgiving attitude of your servant Stephen." (See Acts 6:8-7:60.)

The Final Test

The final test that proves who really heard from God is the end result. In Scripture, there are several instances where a false prophet opposed and attempted to undermine and discredit a true prophet of God. But in the end, God always vindicated and honored His true messenger.

Jeremiah 28:10-17 states:

Then Hananiah the [false] prophet took the yoke from the neck of Jeremiah the [true] prophet and broke it. And Hananiah spoke in the presence of all the people, saying, "Thus says the Lord, 'Even so will I break within two full years, the yoke of Nebuchadnezzar king of Babylon from the neck of all the nations.' " Then the prophet Jeremiah went his way. And the word of the Lord came to Jeremiah, after Hananiah the prophet had broken the yoke from off the neck of the prophet Jeremiah, saying, "Go and speak to Hananiah, saying, 'Thus says the Lord, "You have broken the yokes of wood, but you have made instead of them yokes of iron." For thus says the Lord of hosts, the God of Israel, "I have put a yoke of iron on the neck of all these nations, that they may serve Nebuchadnezzar king of Babylon; and they shall serve him. And I have also given him the beasts of the field." ' " Then Jeremiah the prophet said to Hananiah the prophet, "Listen now, Hananiah, the Lord has not sent you, and you have made this people trust in a lie. Therefore thus says the Lord, 'Behold, I am about to remove you from the face of the earth. This year you are going to die, because you have counseled rebellion against the Lord.' " So Hananiah the prophet died in the same year in the seventh month.

On another occasion, Jeremiah was beaten and put in stocks at the order of the priest Pashhur, chief officer in the temple (Jeremiah 20:1,2), because Jeremiah had pronounced God's upcoming judgment on Jerusalem (Jeremiah 19:15). When Jeremiah was released, the Lord again proclaimed through him judgment on Jerusalem and Judah (Jeremiah 20:3-5). And then Jeremiah prophesied to Pashhur:

And you, Pashhur, and all who live in your house will go into captivity; and you will enter Babylon, and there you will die, and there you will be buried, you and all your friends to whom you have falsely prophesied (Jeremiah 20:6).

After Jeremiah's release from a dungeon in which he would have surely died, and later his rescue from a cistern in which he would have starved to death, he prophesied to King Zedekiah:

If you will not go out to the officers of the king of Babylon, then this city will be given over to the hand of the Chaldeans; and they will burn it with fire, and you yourself will not escape from their hand (Jeremiah 38:18).

We see the tragic fulfillment of this prophecy in Jeremiah chapter 39.

False Peace vs. Impending Judgment

Even though Jeremiah's prophecies of the people being taken into captivity from Jerusalem to Babylon were being fulfilled, Ahab and Zedekiah, two false prophets, continued to prophesy lies. As a result, they were burned in Nebuchadnezzar's fire — not spared like Shadrach, Meshach, and Abednego. Jeremiah 29:20-23 gives the following account of these two false prophets:

> You, therefore, hear the word of the Lord, all you exiles, whom I have sent away from Jerusalem to Babylon. Thus says the Lord of hosts, the God of Israel, concerning Ahab the son of Kolaiah and concerning Zedekiah the son of Maaseiah, who are prophesying to you falsely in My name, "Behold, I will deliver them into the hand of Nebuchadnezzar king of Babylon, and he shall slay them before your eyes. And because of them a curse shall be used by all the exiles from Judah who are in Babylon, saying, 'May the Lord make you like Zedekiah and like Ahab, whom the king of Babylon roasted in the fire, because they have acted foolishly in Israel, and have committed adultery with their neighbors' wives, and have spoken words in My name falsely, which I did not command them; and I am He who knows, and am a witness," declares the Lord.'

Occasionally the Lord has led me to caution or warn individuals or groups concerning unscriptural teachings and practices they are propagating. And after a time of much prayer and fasting, Scripture study, and examining my heart and motives, I would do so. As I look back over the years, I am amazed and humbled that all those who refused to repent have become even more perverse in their teachings and practices and have eventually suffered the consequences.

I have seen the false teachings and the false prophets

come and go. I can somewhat relate to Jeremiah, who after faithfully proclaiming God's Word for many years, questioned King Zedekiah regarding the false prophets:

> Where then are your prophets who prophesied to you, saying, "The king of Babylon will not come against you or against this land" (Jeremiah 37:19)?

Similar to the false prophets of Jeremiah's day who were prophesying peace and prosperity, today's "prophets" continually prophesy renewal, revival, and restoration. But is much of the "revival" occurring today really a commitment to the Christ of the Bible and Biblical Christianity, or is it merely an attraction to all of the excitement and phenomena going on?

Jeremiah accurately prophesied God's impending judgment because of the many sins of the people and their leaders. Then — in contrast to the false peace of the false prophets — Jeremiah prophesied the Lord's promised restoration (Jeremiah 33).

When the judgment prophesied by Jeremiah finally comes upon Judah and Jerusalem, he records his deep distress in the book of Lamentations which clearly shows the consequences of sin and apostasy.

Lamentations 2:2-5 states:

> The Lord has swallowed up; He has not spared all the habitations of Jacob. In His wrath He has thrown down the strongholds of the daughter of Judah; He has brought them down to the ground; He has profaned the kingdom and its princes. In fierce anger He has cut off all the strength of Israel; He has drawn back His right hand from before the enemy. And He has burned in Jacob like a flaming fire consuming round about. He has bent His bow like an enemy, He has set His right hand like an adversary and slain all that were pleasant to the eye; in the tent of the daughter of Zion He has poured out His wrath like fire. The Lord has become like an enemy. He has swallowed up Israel; He has swallowed up all its palaces; He has destroyed its strongholds and multiplied in the daughter of Judah mourning and moaning.

Lamentations 2:13,14 –

How shall I admonish you? To what shall I compare you, O daughter of Jerusalem? To what shall I liken you as I comfort you, O virgin daughter of Zion? For your ruin is as vast as the sea; who can heal you? Your prophets have seen for you false and foolish visions; and they have not exposed your iniquity ....

Lamentations 2:17 –

The Lord has done what He purposed; He has accomplished His word which He commanded from days of old. He has thrown down without sparing, and He has caused the enemy to rejoice over you; He has exalted the might of your adversaries.

Lamentations 4:12,13 –

The kings of the earth did not believe, nor did any of the inhabitants of the world, that the adversary and the enemy could enter the gates of Jerusalem. Because of the sins of her prophets and the iniquities of her priests ....

I believe Scripture strongly indicates a similar end-time scenario of God's judgment on a rebellious world and apostate church (tribulation period), and then Christ's Second Coming and promised restoration of all things.

Lamentations speaks of that hope of restoration in the following verses:

Lamentations 3:21-26, 40 –

This I recall to my mind, therefore I have hope. The Lord's lovingkindnesses indeed never cease, for His compassions never fail. They are new every morning; great is Thy faithfulness. "The Lord is my portion," says my soul, "Therefore I have hope in Him." The Lord is good to those who wait for Him, to the person who seeks Him. It is good that he waits silently for the salvation of the Lord. Let us examine and probe our ways, and let us return to the Lord.

Just as Jeremiah suffered and was persecuted for his obedient testimony for God and for speaking the true word of the Lord, so too, true believers who remain faithful will greatly suffer during the tribulation period because of their testimony for Jesus (the Jesus of the Bible) and the Word of God. In fact, no less than five times does Revelation (in regards to the Apostle John or the persecution of end-time believers who refuse to compromise) mention the utterly crucial and central nature of the Word of God and their testimony for Jesus (Revelation 1:2; 1:9; 6:9; 12:17; 20:4).

A "Spirit" Comes on These People

A "spirit" seems to come on these people once they submit to these false teachings. I have seen several who, after being confronted with the truth yet choosing to continue involvement in a group or church propagating these errors, had a visible countenance change and their hearts became hardened.

These people are being taught a "Christianized fortune-telling." This happened to a woman I knew who had a gentle, loving spirit. She attended one of these "prophets' schools," and after submitting to that teaching immediately began to manifest a spirit of haughtiness and rebellion.

She refused to sit down with me and go through the Scriptures on prophets and personal prophecy or attend a lecture I was giving on the topic, even though I offered her an opportunity to respond. And this woman, who previously (when I was in her favor) had given an unconditional prophecy of blessing for my life and ministry, as well as future persecution, now started prophesying my destruction, and ended up becoming so deceived and vengeful that she became part of that very persecution. Unlike the prophet Nathan who confronted David and prophesied to his face (II Samuel 12:1-14), this supposed prophet (and many others like her) cowardly prophesied my destruction to other people behind my back.

On another occasion a traveling "prophet" stopped by our ministry center. He said the Lord led him to me. After a few minutes of cordial conversation, I informed him that I believed that he and those to whom he was submitted were not speaking the words of the Lord, but were into "Christianized fortune-telling" and speaking from their own inspiration and a counterfeit spirit.

He became irate and said I was young and inexperienced. As he stood up he informed me he was going to prophesy my destruction — thinking I would be intimidated. I said, "Go ahead and prophesy my destruction. But I want to let you know that when you are done, I am going to pray the Lord gives you a double portion of what you prophesy. And then we'll see whose prophecy is fulfilled!" He refused to prophesy in my presence, but hurried out of the ministry center and supposedly prophesied my destruction while in the parking lot. As he pulled away in his motor home, he threw garbage on our property.

Vague Prophecies

Much of what is being accepted as genuine prophecy today is unscriptural nonsense and is being given by those who are speaking from their own inspiration or a demonic counterfeit.

Most of the prophecies I hear today are unimpressive, powerless, and inaccurate. Many are "safe prophecies" — so vague and general that they could be true of almost anyone, like those found in fortune cookies. They are more like psychic readings or fortune-telling than Biblical prophecy.

In contrast, prophecies recorded in Scripture were almost always very specific. Some were fulfilled almost immediately and others were not fulfilled for years or even centuries, but they were precise and exact.

For example:

> Then Joshua made them take an oath at that time, saying, "Cursed before the Lord is the man who rises up and builds this city Jericho; with the loss of his first-born he shall lay its foundation, and with the loss of his youngest son he shall set up its gates" (Joshua 6:26).

This specific prophecy was fulfilled generations later:

> In his days Hiel the Bethelite built Jericho; he laid its foundations with the loss of Abiram his first-born,

and set up its gates with the loss of his youngest son Segub, according to the word of the Lord, which He spoke by Joshua the son of Nun (I Kings 16:34).

Donald C. Stamps, general editor of *The Full Life Study Bible* stated:

> Many of Jeremiah's prophecies were fulfilled in his own lifetime (e.g., Jeremiah 16:9; 20:4; 25:1-14; 27:19-22; 28:15-17; 34:1-5); other prophecies involving the far-distant future were fulfilled later or are yet to be fulfilled (e.g., 23:5-6; 30:8-9; 31:31-34; 33:14-16).[11]

Obedience Prophecies

There are prophecies in Scripture where blessings are promised if the word of the Lord is obeyed. Adverse consequences are promised if it is not obeyed.

Isaiah 1:19,20 states:

> "If you consent and obey, you will eat the best of the land; but if you refuse and rebel, you will be devoured by the sword." Truly, the mouth of the Lord has spoken.

The prophet Jeremiah gave King Zedekiah a choice. If he would obey the word of the Lord and surrender to the King of Babylon, his life would be spared, his family would live, and Jerusalem would not be burned. But if Zedekiah did not obey, then Jerusalem would be handed over to the Babylonians and burned with fire and he would not escape (Jeremiah 38:17,18).

There is a similar prophecy in Jeremiah 42:8-18, which was given to the remnant left in Israel after the Babylonian captivity. They were told that if they stayed in the land, they would be blessed, but if they went to Egypt to reside there they would die by the sword, famine, and plague.

A Call to Repentance

Many prophecies were a call to repentance, such as Isaiah 58:1:

> Cry loudly, do not hold back; raise your voice like a

trumpet, and declare to My people their transgression, and to the house of Jacob their sins.

Joel 2:12-14 states:

"Yet even now," declares the Lord, "Return to Me with all your heart, and with fasting, weeping, and mourning; and rend your heart and not your garments." Now return to the Lord your God, for He is gracious and compassionate, slow to anger, abounding in loving kindness, and relenting of evil. Who knows whether He will not turn and relent, and leave a blessing behind Him ...?

Jonah 1:1,2 commands:

The word of the Lord came to Jonah the son of Amittai saying, "Arise, go to Nineveh the great city, and cry against it, for their wickedness has come up before Me."

Zechariah 7:8-14 admonishes:

Then the word of the Lord came to Zechariah saying, "Thus has the Lord of hosts said, 'Dispense true justice, and practice kindness and compassion each to his brother; and do not oppress the widow or the orphan, the stranger or the poor; and do not devise evil in your hearts against one another.' " But they refused to pay attention, and turned a stubborn shoulder and stopped their ears from hearing. And they made their hearts like flint so that they could not hear the law and the words which the Lord of hosts had sent by His Spirit through the former prophets; therefore great wrath came from the Lord of hosts. "And it came about that just as He called and they would not listen, so they called and I would not listen," says the Lord of hosts; "but I scattered them with a storm wind among all the nations whom they have not known. Thus the land is desolated behind them, so that no one went back and forth, for they made the pleasant land desolate."

Prophecies Must Be 100% Accurate

Not only are most prophecies today usually very vague and general, they are rarely 100% accurate. Many rise up and proclaim: "God told me to say this. God said to go here or to do this. God showed me this is going to happen." But it doesn't come to pass. If a few of their prophecies are fulfilled, these are used to give them credibility, while the prophecies which were proven false are ignored or altered to conform to the circumstances.

Many supposed prophets attempt to whitewash the fact that they are not 100% accurate by stating something like: "A prophet is not a false prophet simply because something he/she says is inaccurate or doesn't seem to apply to us. The prophet may be honest, righteous, and upright, yet immature in his prophesying. Missing it a few times doesn't make one a false prophet. If it did, most preachers and teachers would do best to cease ministering as well."

But that is not Scriptural. Biblical prophecies were amazingly accurate. Prophecies of impending judgment were fulfilled unless the people repented (I Kings 21:27-29; Isaiah 38:1-8; Jeremiah 18:7-10, 26:2-6,12,13; Jonah 3:1-10). Promises were not revoked unless the people were disobedient (I Samuel 2:30).

Although Hananiah, the *false* prophet was not accurate, Jeremiah the *true* prophet was. Jeremiah 28:15-17 says:

> Then Jeremiah the prophet said to Hananiah the prophet, "Listen now, Hananiah, the Lord has not sent you, and you have made this people trust in a lie. Therefore thus says the Lord, 'Behold, I am about to remove you from the face of the earth. This year you are going to die, because you have counseled rebellion against the Lord.' " So Hananiah the prophet died in the same year in the seventh month.

Countless prophecies in Scripture validate this type of accuracy in prophecy — not to mention the amazing fulfillment of specific Messianic prophecies. When a prophet saying, "Thus saith the Lord," is inaccurate, he had better repent. There is a tremendous difference between a counselor saying, "This is my opinion of what you should do," or "This is the Biblical counsel and advice for your situation," and someone saying, "Thus saith the Lord, this is God's direct word to you."

Deuteronomy 18:21,22 states:

And you may say in your heart, "How shall we know the word which the Lord has not spoken?" When a prophet speaks in the name of the Lord, if the thing does not come about or come true, that is the thing which the Lord has not spoken ....

Now if we practiced what they did in the Old Testament times to false prophets, we wouldn't have so many going around saying, "Thus saith the Lord." For Deuteronomy 18:20 warns:

But the prophet who shall speak a word presumptuously in My name which I have not commanded him to speak ... that prophet shall die.

Those who prophesy from their own inspiration will never be 100% accurate unless they merely give very general and vague prophecies. Satan is not omniscient and therefore not 100% accurate, which is why so many of the predictions from those who prophesy through demonic inspiration do not come to pass either.

Isaiah 44:24,25 reveals:

Thus says the Lord, your Redeemer, and the One who formed you from the womb, "I, the Lord, am the maker of all things, stretching out the heavens by Myself, and spreading out the earth all alone, causing the omens of boasters to fail, making fools out of diviners, causing wise men to draw back, and turning their knowledge into foolishness."

In contrast, Scripture says regarding Samuel, one of God's true prophets:

... the Lord was with him and let none of his words fail. And all Israel from Dan even to Beersheba knew that Samuel was confirmed as a prophet of the Lord (I Samuel 3:19,20).

I Samuel 9:6 states:

Behold now, there is a man of God in this city, and the man is held in honor; all that he says surely comes true ....

New Age Channelers

I believe Satan is raising people up today and giving them false prophecies, dreams, and visions to undermine and discredit those who are genuinely hearing from the Lord.

While New Agers are channeling spirits that are proclaiming New Age doctrines, many so-called prophets who claim to be speaking by the Spirit of God are, in my estimation, doing exactly the same thing. They are channels for deceiving spirits who are proclaiming revelations that are amazingly similar to New Age teachings being proclaimed by trance channelers.

After I spoke at a church, a man told me God is continually speaking to him — giving him revelations and prophecies.

He told me "this voice" told him the U.S. would be turned back over to believers and a queen would reign. I told him his scenario was unbiblical and fit more into the reign of Antichrist and the prophesied apostasy. The queen he described sounded like the whore of Babylon in Revelation 18:7:

> To the degree that she glorified herself and lived sensuously, to the same degree give her torment and mourning; for she says in her heart, "I sit as a queen and I am not a widow, and will never see mourning."

Then he said God told him he would see fire come down from heaven. So I opened my Bible to Revelation 13:13 and read:

> And he performs great signs, so that he even makes fire come down out of heaven to the earth in the presence of men.

I told him the only place in the New Testament that talks about fire coming down from heaven is regarding the False Prophet and the Antichrist. It is amazing that what this voice told him was verbatim of what Revelation 13:13 says concerning the Antichrist and the False Prophet.

In reality, this man is a channel for a demon, and doesn't even realize it. I told him that he needed to renounce this voice that was speaking to him — for it was lying and deceiving him. It was not the Spirit of Christ.

I said, "Show me proof that what you are hearing is really from God. Give me Scriptural validation and give me specific fulfillment. Whenever I have said the Lord has spoken to me, I can substantiate it by God's Word and it has always been fulfilled 100%." He had neither validation nor fulfillment, yet he was seeking to sway a church, and if possible, believers in the U.S. by his "revelations from God."

There are countless people like him who are claiming revelations, dreams, visions, and prophecies from God. Most are not only extra-biblical, but contrary to Scripture and have no validation of fulfillment. They also undermine and discredit what God is truly speaking through His genuine servants.

It's More Like Fortune-Telling

I have researched many psychics and fortune-tellers, and there seems to be no apparent difference between their method of prediction and degree of accuracy and that of many so-called prophets of God today. The only difference, seemingly, is that the supposed prophet often uses "Thus saith the Lord."

At a meeting where "holy laughter" was occurring, a woman stood up to give a prophetic utterance. For several minutes she rambled on to the enthusiastic receptivity of the pastor and audience. She called out many ailments that God was supposedly healing (most of which could be true for anyone in the audience) and none of which were documented as being healed. It sounded more like a psychic reading than Biblical prophecy. She also shared for several minutes about the revelation Jesus was supposedly giving her that everyone in the room was being encompassed by light. I thought I was at a New Age gathering — not a Spirit-filled church. When she was done the audience applauded.

One pastor, also known as an apostle, announced at his church that a woman prophetess was coming the next week, so he invited everyone to be sure to come back to get their personal prophecy. They might as well pay ten dollars and go to the local psychic or fortune-teller.

Biblical prophets did not prophesy at will, but when the word of the Lord came to them. Jeremiah 42:7 states, "Now it came about at the end of ten days that the word of the Lord came to Jeremiah." New Testament prophecy also was not determined by the whims of the person operating the gift, but as the Spirit gave utterance.

I saw the following ad in a Christian magazine: "For your personal prophecy send your name, address, and love offering." This resembles fortune-telling far more than any form of prophecy in the Bible. The cassette ordered from this supposed prophet was not only unscriptural in many areas, but was also very boring and unimpressive.

I frequently saw a "Palm Reader" sign in the front yard of a house, and then one day I noticed that the sign was replaced by a new sign that read, "Christian Advisor — Advice on All Matters." Will it next be changed to "Christian Prophet"?

This person probably discovered that palm reading wasn't all that popular, but that there is a gullible market of Christians who don't want to get on their knees and into God's Word to seek His will for their lives.

I was later informed that some Christians helped her change the sign. I hope it was a genuine conversion, but I doubt it very strongly. It was merely a change of terminology. Besides, even if she was converted, she had no business setting herself up that fast as a Christian consultant without time to grow and mature in the Lord.

Meetings where prophets have people line up or call them out and give them a word from the Lord, or meetings where everybody is prophesying over each other, resemble many of the occult and New Age meetings I have researched.

With this in mind, it doesn't surprise me that a supposed prophet of God who was giving personal prophecies to people throughout the country stated that his wife was "at a woman's meeting one day and God got a hold of her and picked her up out of the chair, supernaturally, and threw her on the floor ...."

I have encountered accounts like this in the occult through demonic phenomena, but never of true believers in Scripture.

Putting Personal Prophecies Above God's Word

Although most deny it, the sad reality is that many put the personal prophecies they receive above God's Word. They are encouraged to get a cassette copy of their personal prophecies and write them out and meditate on them and read or listen to them many times.

One noted prophet stated he follows his prophet mentor without question. "Whatever he tells me to do, I do it. I'm not into shepherding. I'm under protection; I have a covering." He may have a covering from that supposed prophet, but he has removed himself from under the Lordship of Jesus Christ.

Deuteronomy 13:1-5 makes known that even if their prophecies come to pass — if they cause you to follow other gods, they are false prophets. At first I thought, "These prophets aren't making anyone go after other gods. They appear to glorify Jesus Christ." But, as I sought the Lord and His Word and researched more, I discovered that their prophecies were getting further and further away from Biblical Christianity. In too many cases they are causing people to go after other gods. They are subtly removing the God of the Bible and Christ's Lordship from their followers' lives and making them dependent on the prophet. They are also replacing the Word of God by encouraging the people to obey, memorize, and conform to personal prophecies and "new revelations" more than God's Word.

So-called prophets of God have prophesied over many separated or divorced people that their spouse would come back to them. Some of these people have waited years. Some even wait for the fulfillment of the prophecy after their former spouse has married someone else — making it unscriptural for them to ever reunite (Deuteronomy 24:4). There is a growing number of casualties — people who have been so hurt, confused, and misled by supposed prophets and prophetic utterances, that they want nothing to do with the true Jesus Christ of the Bible.

Cult Awareness on "New Revelations"

It is sad to discover that what I had written many years ago about the cults concerning "new revelations" is relevant for the Church today. The following excerpts are from my *Cult Awareness* booklet:

Although they say their "new revelation" merely sheds additional light on what God has already revealed through the Scriptures, in reality, it adds to or subtracts from the Bible. Ultimately, their extra-biblical revelation is given greater authority and importance than the Bible.

It is interesting to note that most cult leaders who have received "new revelations" have acknowledged receiving them during encounters with spirit beings. A look behind the scenes will reveal a definite association with the occult and contact with demonic beings who masquerade as angelic beings, spirits of the dead, or even Christ Himself.

Now realize, a cult leader who is attempting to gain followers for his "new revelation" is usually not so naive as to immediately attempt to persuade "Christians" to accept his/her "extreme" ideas and beliefs. Instead, they will give some general truths that almost everyone agrees with and talk about God, Christ, the Bible, miracles, etc. The immature and unsuspecting listener is impressed. Very subtly the cultist reveals his "new revelation" of false doctrine mixed with just enough truth to keep you off guard. Finally the cultist reveals that his true allegiance is to some book or teaching other than the Bible and someone other than Jesus Christ.

Cultists are usually successful in proclaiming their "new truth" to those who have little of the "old truth." But in reality their message is not new at all. Ecclesiastes 1:9,10 states, "... there is nothing new under the sun. Is there anything of which one might say, 'See this, it is new'? Already it has existed for ages which were before us."

So although they claim to have God's "new revelation" for the world, it is really just new names and disguises for Satan's old methods of leading people away from the God of the Bible and from His revealed truth in Jesus Christ.

At a time when thousands of New Age messiahs and prophets are attempting to gain followers for their "new revelations," Galatians 1:8 warns, "But even though we, or an angel from heaven, should preach to you a gospel contrary to that which we have preached to you, let him be accursed."[12]

Evaluate All Things in the Light of Scripture

When problems concerning issues and new teachings arose in the early New Testament Church, believers evaluated them in light of Old Testament Scripture. For example, in Acts 15:13-19, James uses Old Testament Scripture to provide the Apostles' conclusion regarding the Gospel being proclaimed to the Gentiles.

So too, in these last days, we must evaluate all so-called prophecies and "new revelations" in light of Scripture. When they run contrary to Scripture, no matter how good they sound, no matter how anointed they seem, we must reject them. If we don't, we will soon be following "another Jesus," not the actual Jesus of the Bible; "a different spirit," not the true Holy Spirit; and "a different gospel," not the genuine Biblical Gospel (II Corinthians 11:4).

In a personal letter from David Wilkerson, pastor of Times Square Church, he writes, "Personally, I never stray from the Word and I do not give much credence to much of what is called personal prophecy and new revelation. Ninety-nine percent of it is zeal without wisdom, repetitious, and absolutely nothing new except error. We are safest when we stay rock solid on the Word."

There is a Need for Biblical Balance

I Corinthians 14:29-33 admonishes:

And let two or three prophets speak, and let the others pass judgment. But if a revelation is made to another who is seated, let the first keep silent. For you can all prophesy one by one, so that all may learn and all may be exhorted; and the spirits of prophets are subject to prophets. For God is not a God of confusion but of peace, as in all the churches of the saints.

I Thessalonians 5:19-21 gives us what I believe to be one of the most balanced Scriptures on prophecy. It states:

Do not quench the Spirit; do not despise prophetic utterances. But examine everything carefully; hold fast to that which is good.

We have an obligation to allow the manifestation of the gifts of the Spirit, but you and I have a responsibility to evaluate them in light of Scripture and to reject that which is not in accord with God's Word — and to hold fast to that which is good. In contradiction of this Scripture, we are seeing raised up in our midst self-proclaimed and man-appointed prophets who refuse to be judged. Through their twisting of God's Word, they are making it almost impossible for anyone to Biblically critique or evaluate them.

They are not allowing us to be like the Berean Christians who were commended for receiving the Word eagerly and for searching out everything to make certain the teachings were accurate (Acts 17:11). As a result, there is rampant false teaching on crucial Biblical doctrines being accepted under the guise of inspired prophecies and "new revelations."

These supposed modern-day prophets and apostles are wrongly attempting to manipulate their followers into believing they are above questioning. While Jesus did rebuke the church of Ephesus for leaving its first love, He commended it in Revelation 2:2 for not enduring evil men, and for putting to the test those who call themselves apostles, but who are false.

I Believe in Prophecy

I believe the gift of prophecy is for today. The Church needs to be encouraged, corrected, and built up with messages from the very heart of God — brought forth by

His Spirit, and found in His Word. True Biblical prophecy is accurately proclaiming "Thus saith the Lord." The genuine word of the Lord today will always be in harmony with His written revelation to man, the Holy Scriptures.

Biblical prophecy is not merely foretelling future events, but often *forthtelling* the very heart and mind of God. Revelation 19:10 states, "... For the testimony of Jesus is the spirit of prophecy." Biblical prophecy is not going to exalt and magnify and make you dependent on the person operating the gift; it will exalt and glorify and draw you to the Jesus of the Bible!

Concerning true prophecy in the Church, Scripture states:

> ... if an unbeliever or an ungifted man enters, he is convicted by all, he is called to account by all; the secrets of his heart are disclosed; and so he will fall on his face and worship God, declaring that God is certainly among you (I Corinthians 14: 24,25).

But too much of what is going on in Christian circles today is not the genuine gift of prophecy by proclaiming the true word of the Lord under the anointing of His Spirit. It is a poor imitation, false prophecy, and "Christianized fortune-telling." It is prophesying from one's own inspiration, and often it is a demonic counterfeit.

I challenge you! Do not accept as genuine a prophecy or revelation from anyone, unless it is in exact accord with God's Word, is 100% accurate, confirms what His Spirit has already spoken to your heart, truly exalts the Jesus Christ of the Bible, and draws you closer to Him.

Never accept anyone's prophecies and revelations as a higher authority than the Bible or make anyone the director of your life (except Jesus Christ), or run to other people for quick prophetic advice, when you should be seeking guidance from God's Word and allowing God's Spirit to speak to your own heart. Get on your knees and seek His face and obediently follow His Word and Spirit!

Should Our Experience Go Beyond God's Word?

Over the years I have worked closely with Jim Weikal, Biblical Research and Instruction Director, and have been pleased by his desire to know and defend Biblical Christianity. This chapter, therefore, was written by Jim at my request.

Many leaders in the church today use experience and feelings to negate clear Scriptural mandates, encouraging people to ignore the teachings of Scripture and to embrace "a new move of God." Multitudes of people are, therefore, embracing beliefs, practices, and phenomena that are not only extra-biblical but are also contrary to Scripture.

A sincere eagerness to see the Holy Spirit manifest Himself in a mighty way has led to a very faulty method of evaluation — personal experience and emotion. The idea that adherence to the Word of God would offend the Holy Spirit, and therefore quench Him, is human speculation and incorrect. Liberal theologians, cult movements, ecumenical movements, and the like disdain the notion of Biblical authority because it destroys their distorted views and spirit of compromise. In the book of Revelation the saints are martyred for their commitment to the Word.

> And when He broke the fifth seal, I saw underneath the altar the souls of those who had been slain **because of the Word of God,** and because of the testimony which they had maintained (Revelation 6:9).

> And I saw the souls of those who had been beheaded because of the testimony of Jesus and

because of the Word of God (Revelation 20:4). (Also see Revelation 1:2,9 and 12:17.)

To discern properly whether a supernatural move is from God or the adversary, we must apply the Scriptures.

> Be diligent to present yourself approved to God as a workman who does not need to be ashamed, handling accurately the Word of truth (II Timothy 2:15).

To correctly handle the Word of truth requires years of hard work — time, study, memorization, commitment, discipline, vigilance, and the like. It is written:

> All Scripture is inspired by God and profitable for teaching, for reproof, for correction, for training in righteousness (II Timothy 3:16).

The Bible is clear on the issue of faith and practice. More than 70 times the phrases "it is written" or "according to the Word" are used when the author wishes to show authority for his position.

Why do people insist on calling Jesus "Lord, Lord" and then not do what He says? Why do people say they diligently study the Scriptures and love the Lord, but when the Scriptures show no validation for much of today's spiritual phenomena, proponents say, "This is a new move of the Spirit that goes beyond the Word of God"? They ignore the lack of Biblical support.

When Jesus came into the world, He did not ask the Jews if they felt He was the Messiah. He used references to prophecy:

> Now He said to them, "These are My words which I spoke to you while I was still with you, that all things which are written about Me in the Law of Moses and the Prophets and the Psalms must be fulfilled" (Luke 24:44).

He expected those listening to Him to search the Scriptures. Why should we do any differently? Has the body of Christ totally forgotten Paul's warning about the last days?:

> Let no one in any way deceive you, for it will not come unless the apostasy comes first, and the man of lawlessness is revealed, the son of destruction (II Thessalonians 2:3).

There is an apostasy from the faith "which was once for all delivered to the saints" (Jude 3). Jesus asked in Luke 18:8, "... when the Son of Man comes, will He find faith on the earth?"

Jesus was speaking of faith in Him. Unfortunately, many will answer, "Yes." But their faith will be in false christs, false prophets, false signs, false wonders, and false miracles!

Is the body of Christ so deficient in Biblical discernment that any supernatural experience can be perceived as coming from God simply because leaders say it is, or the experience feels so good it has to be from God?

We are given in the book of Acts, chapters 2 and 4, an account of the greatest revival in New Testament times, where the 3,000 and 5,000 were added to the church. In neither of these instances is there information given of any unusual happenings by the converts themselves.

To come against the Holy Spirit is dangerous, and I don't know of any true Christian who wants to knowingly do that. But, on the other hand, I don't know of any Christian who knowingly wants to embrace a false or demonic spirit during worship. To know the difference we must have the authority contained in the Bible.

When advocating that Scripture is the standard for evaluating spiritual matters and not experience or feelings, many Biblical references can be found:

1. **a)** "Why do Your disciples transgress the tradition of the elders? For they do not wash their hands when they eat bread." And He answered and said to them, "And why do you yourselves **transgress the commandment of God for the sake of your tradition?**" (Matthew 15:2,3).

   b) He was also saying to them, "You nicely **set aside the commandment of God in order to keep your tradition**" (Mark 7:9).

To evaluate Scripture based simply on what tradition says or on some experience of the past is dangerous. Just because something occurred in the past does not automatically make it right. To refer back to revivals and say, "Well it happened then, so it must be OK now," is using a faulty method of getting at the truth. For if what was done then was wrong, it is just as wrong now. Don't set aside Scripture for the sake of sensations.

2. And when they say to you, "Consult the mediums and the spiritists who whisper and mutter," should not a people consult their God? Should they consult the dead on behalf of the living? To the law and to the testimony! **If they do not speak according to this Word,** it is because they have no dawn (Isaiah 8:19,20).

Even in the time of the prophet Isaiah, the law and the testimony were the standards for judging belief and practice.

3. But we have renounced the things hidden because of shame, not walking in craftiness or **adulterating the Word of God,** but by the manifestation of truth commending ourselves to every man's conscience in the sight of God (2 Corinthians 4:2).

The Word of God should not have to be distorted or twisted to advance some belief or practice. Let the truth of God's Word speak to the issue and judge accordingly.

4. I testify to everyone who hears the words of the prophecy of this book: **if anyone adds to them,** God shall add to him the plagues which are written in this book; and **if anyone takes away from the words of the book of this prophecy,** God shall take away his part from the tree of life and from the holy city, which are written in this book (Revelation 22:18,19).

People who are saying that God is doing a new move which goes beyond His Word are standing on dangerous ground.

5. The Lord your God will raise up for you a prophet like me from among you, from your countrymen, you shall listen to Him. This is according to all that you asked of the Lord your God in Horeb on the day of the assembly, saying, "Let me not hear again the voice of the Lord my God, let me not see this great fire anymore, lest I die." And the Lord said to me, "They have spoken well. I will raise up a Prophet from among their countrymen like you, and I will put My words in His mouth, and He shall speak to them all that I command Him. And it

shall come about that whoever will not listen to My words which He shall speak in My name, I Myself will require it of him" (Deuteronomy 18:15-19).

Notice in the next verse that Jesus rebuked the Jews for not believing what had been written about Him:

> For if you believed Moses, you would believe Me; **for he wrote of Me** (John 5:46).

6. These next two verses point to the same concept — understand what the Scriptures say and act according to their teachings.

> Now on the last day, the great day of the feast, Jesus stood and cried out, saying, "If any man is thirsty, let him come to Me and drink. He who believes in Me, **as the Scripture said,** 'From his innermost being shall flow rivers of living water' " (John 7:37,38).

Notice the reaction of the people:

> **On hearing His words,** some of the people said, "Surely this man is the Prophet" (John 7:40 NIV).

7. This is the Moses who said to the sons of Israel, "God shall raise up for you a Prophet like me from your brethren" (Acts 7:37).

Stephen used the Scriptures to prove his beliefs just before he was martyred (Acts 7).

8. And after the **reading of the Law and the Prophets** the synagogue officials sent to them, saying, "Brethren, if you have any word of exhortation for the people, say it." (Acts 13:15).

Continuing in verse 16 of Acts chapter 13, Paul addresses the Jews at Antioch about Jesus Christ. Paul begins by relating historical facts from the Scriptures the Jews knew so well — the stay in Egypt, the wandering in the desert, the period of the judges and the kings, and the promise of a Savior. When Paul gets to the preaching of John the Baptist and Jesus' life, death, and resurrection, he shows how Scripture has been fulfilled by quoting from the Psalms and the Prophets. Paul used historical facts and Scriptural truth to authenticate his reasoning.

We need to understand that any line of reasoning takes us down some path. If our reasoning begins with man's experience and emotion as the basis for determining God's truth, that path will lead to apostasy. Emotion and experience are important to the spiritual life, and God wants worshippers with passion and feeling toward Him. But without a Biblical starting point and Scriptural "guardrails" on both sides, the believer is headed down a meandering, hazard-filled path paved with confusion, delusion, and doctrinal error.

Consider the following passages:

> And according to Paul's custom, he went to them, and for three Sabbaths **reasoned with them from the Scriptures, explaining and giving evidence** that the Christ had to suffer and rise again from the dead, and saying, "This Jesus whom I am proclaiming to you is the Christ." And some of them were persuaded and joined Paul and Silas, along with a great multitude of the God-fearing Greeks and a number of the leading women (Acts 17:2-4).

> And the brethren immediately sent Paul and Silas away by night to Berea; and when they arrived, they went into the synagogue of the Jews. Now these were more noble-minded than those in Thessalonica, for they received the word with great eagerness, **examining the Scripture daily, to see whether these things were so** (Acts 17:10,11).

The message of Jesus, Stephen, Paul, and other leaders of the early church is loud and clear: The Scriptures are the final authority in spiritual affairs — not feelings, emotions, intuition, past revivals, personal testimonies, manipulation, prophecies, movements, or the enthusiastic crowd.

I want to thank Jim Weikal, Biblical Research and Instruction Director, for contributing this timely and significant chapter. As Christians seeking a Biblical lifestyle, God's Word must remain central to our experience.

False Signs and Miracles –
"Holy Laughter," "Drunk in the Spirit," ...

Just like in the days of Jesus (Luke 11:29), today's generation wants to see signs and wonders. As a result, they will follow almost any spiritual leader who promises the "miraculous."

Now there is nothing wrong with feelings, emotions, and excitement, for these can be valid responses to the genuine moving of God's Spirit. Moreover, we are not to quench the Spirit who desires to work in our lives in a real and special way. The danger arises when people begin seeking experiences, miracles, signs, and revelations more than they seek the Lord and His Word, or when they allow unbiblical phenomena to occur.

I certainly realize that many churches could surely use a little more excitement and enthusiasm. Some are so dead and cold that you feel like you're at a funeral home. But many churches have gone to the opposite extreme and have a lot of sensationalism and emotionalism, but little discernment and knowledge of God's Word. They have replaced the message of the Gospel with a "show."

Somewhere between the boring, loveless, and lifeless

church, and the church that specializes in miracles and the supernatural, is the Biblically balanced church. We need to allow God's Spirit to move in a dynamic and exciting way. But we must remember, the same Apostle Paul who demonstrated the exciting power of the resurrected Christ also warned against false teachers, counterfeit miracles, and the misuse of the gifts of the Holy Spirit.

I Believe in the Gifts of the Spirit

After I spoke at a Full Gospel banquet, a woman came up to me and said, "You are so refreshing to hear because I see so much error and deception today. It's exciting to see someone like you who believes in the gifts of the Spirit, but who is also warning about the counterfeit and the fakery going on. We need to have that kind of balance and credibility."

I believe in the gifts of the Spirit. I have seen genuine healings and miracles through faith in Christ. In fact, in an upcoming book entitled, *The Impossible*, I am documenting some of the miraculous interventions the Lord has done in my life and ministry.

I have seen the genuine power and moving of God's Spirit. I have also seen the imitation of flesh, and the demonic counterfeit. Experience-oriented people who lack discernment and who allow phenomena to determine their beliefs, instead of properly interpreting and lining up their experiences with the Word of God, are easy prey for exploitation and counterfeit experiences which they accept as genuinely from God.

Purpose of the Spirit

One of the main purposes of the Holy Spirit is to empower God's people to boldly and effectively witness for the truth of Christ (Acts 1:8; John 15:26). The gifts of the Spirit are to exalt Christ and to draw people to Him — *not* to draw attention to the person operating the gift. A major purpose of miracles is to confirm and validate the truth of the messenger (II Corinthians 12:12) and the message being proclaimed. Acts 14:3 says:

> Therefore they spent a long time there speaking boldly with reliance upon the Lord, who was bearing witness to the Word of His grace, granting that signs and wonders be done by their hands.

The gifts of the Holy Spirit are also to exhort and strengthen the body of Christ — but not so believers can merely have a "good time" enjoying exotic, bizarre, and often useless displays of supernatural power. More than signs and wonders, my heart's desire is for the Holy Spirit's presence in power to bring deep conviction (I Thessalonians 1:5) on the hearts of those who hear me proclaim God's Word. I want to be used to turn the hearts of the people to the Lord and to motivate them to walk in faithfulness until He returns.

The Holy Spirit convicts (exposes and convinces) the world concerning sin, righteousness, and judgment (John 16:8). *The Full Life Study Bible* footnote on this matter states:

> Through the manifestation of the Spirit among God's people, sin will be exposed, repentance called for, and sinners convicted. Where there is no exposing of unrighteousness, no conviction of sin or no plea for repentance, the Holy Spirit is clearly not at work according to the Biblical pattern. [13]

Most Are a Poor Imitation or Counterfeit

When I read in Scripture the message Paul, Peter, and John proclaimed, it is far different from much of what is being heard today. And most "miracles" today don't resemble at all the miracles God performed in the early Church as recorded in Acts.

From research, studying God's Word, and knowing God's Spirit (through prayer and fasting), I must conclude that much of what is being passed off today as the Holy Spirit is a very poor imitation. It reminds me more of an energy force or spirit guide, than the Holy Spirit of the Bible.

While there are some churches who are experiencing

a genuine movement of God's Spirit, I do not believe the Church today has *really* witnessed the *full* outpouring of God's Spirit. Even though I have seen the Lord do some incredible things, I have to admit that we are not seeing an outpouring of God's Spirit today like those who witnessed them in the book of Acts and in the prophecies of the second chapter of Joel.

I have traveled throughout the world, and much of what I see is imitation. It's emotionalism, hype, the power of suggestion. It's psychological manipulation, mass hysteria, psychosomatic. Some of it is even outright fakery, or worse yet, a demonic counterfeit.

Leaders "Perform" to Keep Excitement

And one of the reasons that it's happening is because those in leadership, who do not have the genuine moving of God's Spirit, feel tremendous pressure to "perform" to keep the church growing and excited. As a result, many Christian leaders succumb by turning to gimmicks, emotionalism, and even using New Age and occultic techniques to "create" spiritual experiences and excitement.

Phillip Keller writes concerning much of these phenomena in his book *Predators In Our Pulpits:*

> The main objective is simply to satisfy the crowds. Their demand for an exciting experience ... must be met. The end result is that millions of earnest, seeking souls have been given a bowl full of sensationalism but scarcely a crumb of truth. They come with searching spirits that can only be truly satisfied by the presence of the Living Christ. They go away deceived into believing that they have been touched by God's Spirit when in fact it was largely a sham and show ....

> An even more serious dimension of their spiritual deception lies in the fact that they are often led to believe a lie. Exciting revelations, stimulating prophecies, erotic encounters (often counterfeited by false teaching), and spurious spirits lead the gullible ones ....[14]

Usurping the Place of the Holy Spirit

Christian leaders who are involved in any way in attempting to "create" spiritual experiences for their followers must realize they are not helping God; they are usurping the place of the Holy Spirit. They are powerless before the Lord and they know it, so they turn to these other techniques to make people think they really do have power. But I have traveled in too many Christian circles and have seen too many things, both in front of and behind the scenes, to be gullible about this kind of inferior phenomena.

Satan is deceiving many Christians into accepting a pseudo spiritual experience so they will be desensitized and not *truly* seek the Lord for the genuine outpouring of His Spirit. I think the hoopla camouflages their lack of the real power of the Holy Spirit, and their external manifestations act as a smoke screen to hide their lack of internal commitment to the Christ of Scripture.

It Mirrored the Shallow, Wild Times of the World

As a brand-new Christian in 1971, I got caught up in a group of some supposed super spiritual Christians, which specialized in all the signs and wonders. So-called supernatural phenomena such as healings, being slain in the Spirit, miracles, laughing and dancing in the Spirit, revelations, personal prophecies, angelic encounters, visions, casting demons out of Christians, and vomiting up demons were the norm.

Having just given up my former wild lifestyle in the world, it was most appealing to discover (or so I thought) that I could replace it with a wild lifestyle of continual miracles and the supernatural. But I soon discovered that most of the people in this group were too busy seeking all the excitement and the signs and wonders to have time to seek the Lord through prayer and fasting and diligently studying His Word. As a result, they lacked the necessary spiritual discernment and Scripture knowledge to see that they were into beliefs and practices that were contrary to God's Word and definitely not of His Spirit.

Besides, their walk with the Lord was like a yo-yo. When the supposed miracles and ecstatic experiences were happening to them, they loved the Lord, but when they were not, they quickly fell away. Today, almost all of this group is far away from the Lord because they built their walk on emotions, excitement, and the sensational, rather than the Scriptural principles of commitment, obedience, and discipline.

I quickly realized that just as the wild parties and getting high before accepting Christ were only short-lived pleasures for me, so too, this hyper-emotional lifestyle did not bring the long-lasting spiritual fulfillment I desired. The only way to be totally fulfilled spiritually is to desire the Lord with all your heart, and to walk in obedience to His Word and Spirit. As a result, I would soon witness His miraculous power, but not the pseudo miracles and carnival atmosphere of before. It also would not be by my initiation, but by His sovereign intervention.

As I reflect back on the highlights of my life and ministry, I am aware of the many miracles the Lord has done. By focusing on these miracles out of context with the rest of my life, it might seem as though I experienced constant miracles. However, sometimes I went for weeks or even months through a wilderness where God molded and trained me without any apparent supernatural interventions. In the same way, if you take Scripture out of context when looking at the lives of Daniel, Moses, Elijah, Paul, and others, it may seem like they had constant miracles. The total picture, however, shows this not to be true.

Psychosomatic Healings

To maintain integrity in the body of Christ, I must also say that many of those bragging about having a healing ministry today are merely doing psychosomatic healings — not genuine divine healing.

A world-famous evangelist spoke for over two hours

yet quoted only a few Scriptures. The rest of the time he talked about his experiences and his vision from the Lord.

The affirmative statements he had everyone repeat about their being blessed were almost like chanting, and many seemed to be in an altered state of consciousness (and almost a trance-like state) as they repeated them.

During the altar call he had many raise both of their hands high in the air. Then he would hit them on their foreheads. Some wobbled and a few fell down.

There were also some supposed healings, but they were merely psychosomatic. The two who were in wheelchairs left unchanged, as did all the others who had chronic afflictions.

I also heard another popular evangelist who frequently bragged about his healing ministry. At a national convention I attended, there were many supposed healings, but once again they were psychosomatic. A woman who was brought in on an ambulance cot and others like her left the same way they came.

Blatantly False Healings

The national secretary of a well-respected movement in India with over 2,000 churches told me that he never saw one genuine healing in India by all the so-called healing evangelists that came through. He told me that an American evangelist recently had a big healing crusade in India. Thousands of dollars were spent on posters, advertising, and feeding people after the services to draw big crowds. He said several people in India were paid to come and fake healings and then testify how they were healed.

The evangelist told people to raise one hand if they had any prayer requests. At the very moment they raised their hands, his staff would shoot photographs to bring back to the U.S. of all the raised hands claiming that these people were in the process of giving their lives to Jesus. Then he would ask them to raise two hands, photograph them with their hands in the air, and claim to his supporters back home that these people were praising the Lord.

The national secretary said to me, "It was all fake!" A militant Hindu group brought 10 blind and crippled people and told this evangelist they would give 10,000 U.S. dollars if he healed just one of them, but the evangelist wouldn't even pray for them.

The national secretary said he sees no lasting fruit from all these "miracle" crusades. All the people want is the excitement — very few want true salvation. He also said there were demon-possessed people writhing around on the floor like snakes, but the evangelist didn't even bother with them.

At a crusade in Nigeria, a minister prayed loud and emotionally with those who came forward. He pushed on their heads and most of them fell over backwards, supposedly falling under the power of God. But it was proven to be all emotion and hype. Immediately after a teenage girl was "slain in the Spirit," a 10-year-old blind girl who had no eyes in her sockets was brought up for prayer for a healing. After this minister yelled and hollered and pushed on her head, guess what happened? Nothing! She left the same way she came.

The same Spirit which had allegedly knocked down all those people surely could have also restored the girl's eyes. But God's Spirit was not doing it. It was merely hype and emotion.

I have witnessed this happen over and over. Sure, there are many claims of healings — but either the claims were not verifiable, or the healings were merely psychosomatic. I have not discovered even one legitimate healing of the type performed by Jesus or Paul or Peter to be associated with this phenomenon or by so-called faith healers. In fact, the ones operating this supposed gift from God almost always avoid the people who obviously need a real supernatural touch from the Lord if they are going to *truly* be healed. But the time is coming when false prophets and false messiahs will perform great signs and counterfeit miracles (Matthew 24:24).

Compare Today's Show With Our Lord's Example

While imitators "perform miracles" to impress people, Jesus did so out of compassion and to the glory of God. His miracles were a sign and validation of His message and Messianic claims. Jesus and the apostles did not go around merely healing "invisible" ailments such as headaches, high blood pressure, heart palpitations, back pain, etc. They healed "visible" organic disease — blind eyes, lepers, palsy, the lame, paralytics, withered hands, a severed ear, and the like. They even raised the dead. Those healed in Scripture did not have to confess, claim, or visualize their healing before it occurred. The healings of Jesus were usually immediate, complete, irreversible, and undeniable even to His opponents.

When we think of the "miracles" performed by today's faith healers, could we honestly say what Nicodemus said to Jesus:

> Rabbi, we know that You have come from God ... for no one can do these signs that You do unless God is with him (John 3:2).

Those whom the Lord is really using in supernatural healings do very little boasting about it. You won't find these people advertising their gift in Christian magazines or on radio or television. They're out serving the Lord in places and ways through which they won't get much worldly credit. One day they will receive the Lord's reward for their faithfulness and for allowing His power to be manifested through their lives — without attempting to use it to exalt themselves, advance their own ministries, or receive financial blessings.

"Slain in the Spirit"

As a new Christian I was very open to being "slain in the Spirit," but I was not the type who would be pushed or go down on my own. Many who had this phenomenon manifest in their ministries would lay hands on me, expecting the power of God to knock me down. Some even had me close my eyes and raise my hands and then pushed hard against my forehead so as to be certain I went down, but I never went down. I know those who endorse this phenomenon might say, "Well, you didn't go down because you resisted." But that's not true; I was very much open to it. I'm just not easily influenced or affected by such emotionalism (and sometimes actually demonic phenomena).

If it really were the power of God's Spirit which had "slain" these people, then He could also drop them unhurt to the ground without the need for catchers. And they should get up off the floor either as changed people or being genuinely healed.

David Wilkerson said it well: "If people are going to fall down, I want to see them falling under the conviction of the Holy Ghost. And the vision I want them to receive is a renewed vision of Jesus. And the manifestation I want them to have is their rising from the floor as a new creature in Christ!" [15]

In Scripture, believers **fell on their faces** in awe and worship before the Lord (Abraham – Genesis 17:1-3; Joshua 5:13-15; Ezekiel 1:28; 3:23; 43:1-5; 44:4; Daniel 8:15-18,27; 10:7-11; disciples at transfiguration – Matthew 17:5,6; angels and elders – Revelation 7:11; 11:16,17). And the experience happened directly between God and the individual — no human being had to lay hands on them, and none fell after being blown on.

Even the book that deals extensively with end-time prophecy, the book of Revelation, nowhere states anything about being "slain in the Spirit," receiving "holy laughter," or "dancing in the Spirit." Even when one was in the very presence of God, there is no such case mentioned. But there are several accounts in Revelation of His people who by their own volition **fall on their faces** to worship Him in awe and reverence (Revelation 4:9,10; 7:11; 11:16).

Stand Up on Your Feet

Those who experience being "slain in the Spirit" not only usually fall backwards (which contradicts all Biblical accounts for believers), but they also frequently lie there for several minutes to several hours doing "carpet time" while the Lord supposedly speaks to them and ministers to them.

Many of the Scriptural accounts which proponents use to endorse "slain in the Spirit" are taken out of context. Scriptural records indicate that the Lord often tells those overwhelmed by His presence to **get up** before He speaks to them. The following examples of Scripture bear this out:

Ezekiel 1:28 - 2:2 –

As the appearance of the rainbow in the clouds on a rainy day, so was the appearance of the surrounding radiance. Such was the appearance of the likeness of the glory of the Lord. And when I saw it, I fell on my face and heard a voice speaking. Then He said to me, "Son of man, **stand on your feet** that I may speak with you!" And as He spoke to me the Spirit entered me and set me on my feet; and I heard Him speaking to me.

Ezekiel 3:23, 24 –

So I got up and went out to the plain; and behold, the glory of the Lord was standing there, like the glory which I saw by the River Chebar, and I fell on my face. The Spirit then entered me and **made me stand on my feet ....**

Matthew 17:6,7 –

And when the disciples heard this, they fell on their faces and were much afraid. And Jesus came to them and touched them and said, "**Arise,** and do not be afraid."

(Also see Ezekiel 43:1-5; Daniel 8:15-18; 10:7-11; and Acts 9:3-8)

There is no record in Scripture of believers "falling under the power of the Spirit" when Jesus or the apostles laid hands on them and prayed for them. Yet in charismatic circles people line up to have hands laid on them in order to receive this euphoric experience.

If the Scriptures given by proponents of "slain in the Spirit" to validate their phenomenon are taken in their proper context, you will see that what is happening in their experience today is as far removed from the Biblical accounts as a backyard carnival is from Disneyland.

It is apparent from evaluating Scripture in context, extensive research, and personal observation, that this phenomenon as it usually occurs today is not Scriptural. There are many possible reasons for its occurrence ranging from the power of suggestion, conditioning, and peer pressure to be "slain" lest one be considered less spiritual, to loss of balance, mind control, mass hypnosis, and sometimes demonic manifestation (the possession-trance-state of shamanism).

"Holy Laughter"

Just as there is no real Scriptural support for being "slain in the Spirit," there is no Scriptural basis for the phenomenon called "holy laughter."

I'm all for "the joy of the Lord" (Nehemiah 8:10), and I'm well aware that "a joyful heart is good medicine" (Proverbs 17:22). There is nothing wrong with laughing and being joyful. "Holy laughter," however, is a dangerous deception.

"Holy Ghost bartenders" serve the "new wine" of "holy laughter" and encourage people to "belly-on-up to the bar." Adherents are told to surrender to the laughter (I thought we should only surrender to the Lord) and just "let go."

People fall on the floor convulsed in uncontrollable laughter or giggling — sometimes for hours. Some laugh hysterically while others cry. Some roll around on the floor. Some dance "sensually." Others have out-of-body experiences and claim to have seen visions or angels. I have also seen participants (many being pastors) jerking, shaking violently, roaring like lions, barking like dogs, and hissing and writhing like snakes — definite occultic phenomena. Hours later, some stagger out of the church or laugh uncontrollably while driving down the road.

This bizarre phenomenon is fed by a major misconception that needs to be brought to light. Many supposedly Spirit-filled Christians believe and teach today that being filled with the Spirit produces the same effect on a person as being drunk on wine. This just isn't so!

The irrational behavior mentioned above has

absolutely no Scriptural basis. In fact, Ephesians 5:18, one of the passages used most often in support of this kind of experience, actually means the exact opposite of what is being propagated and taught in this false movement.

Trusting and immature Christians are being erroneously led to believe that because this text says that Christians should not get drunk on wine, but should be filled with the Spirit, that it means "don't get drunk on wine, get drunk on the Spirit." However, based on research done as part of an exegetical study in the original Greek language on Ephesians 5:18 and 19, David Sabella concludes:

> When the verse is examined within its Scriptural context and with an understanding of the historical and cultural background into which it was written, it is obvious that Paul is here calling for sobriety and *not* intoxication of any kind. He is commanding the Church not to worship as the hellenistic cultists. Once drunk on wine, they would work themselves into a degrading and orgiastic state to worship the false pagan god Dionysus. Paul is contrasting their trumped-up, wine-induced frenzies of religious exaltation with the sober, orderly, and controlled worship that being filled with the Spirit brings. The meaning of being filled with the Spirit, therefore, is not to get "drunk in the Spirit," but rather the very opposite. It is a call to discipline and self-control. These two ideas are mutually incompatible, not similar.[16]

The *Interpreter's Bible* states it this way:

> The antithesis is not between **wine** and **spirit** but between the two states — intoxication with its degrading effects on the one hand; and a [sober] progressive fulfillment of the spiritual life on the other.[17]

Why Not "Drunk" in Acts 2:15 and Ephesians 5:18?

A highly speculative and faulty interpretation of being "drunk in the Spirit," based on taking Acts 2:15 and Ephesians 5:18 out of context, has resulted in false teachings.

Consider Acts 2:15

Ten days after Christ's ascension, while the 120 were praying and worshipping the Lord in an upper room in Jerusalem, a mighty rushing wind came and tongues of fire rested on the heads of the 120. They were all filled with the Holy Spirit and began to speak with other tongues as the Spirit gave them utterance. So why did some in the crowd think the 120 were drunk?

Notice, it was not because they were staggering, falling down, or laughing uncontrollably in an inebriated state. The answer given in Acts 2:5-13 is this:

> Now there were Jews living in Jerusalem, devout men, from every nation under heaven. And when this sound occurred, the multitude came together, and were bewildered, because they were each one hearing them speak in his own language. And they were amazed and marveled, saying, "Why, are not all these who are speaking Galileans? And how is it that we each hear them in our own language to which we were born? Parthians and Medes and Elamites, and residents of Mesopotamia, Judea and Cappadocia, Pontus and Asia, Phrygia and Pamphylia, Egypt and the districts of Libya around Cyrene, and visitors from Rome, both Jews and proselytes, Cretans and Arabs — we hear them in our own tongues speaking of the mighty deeds of God." And they continued in amazement and great perplexity, saying to one another, "What does this mean?" But others were mocking and saying, "They are full of sweet wine."

Why were most of the multitude of devout men from every nation bewildered and amazed? Because they heard foreigners declaring the wonders of God in their own tongues (Acts 2:5-12).

Notice, it was the mockers who said they had too much wine (Acts 2:13). The mockers, not the multitude, falsely accused the others of being drunk because, while some heard their own language, they also heard other languages. To the mockers this sounded like babbling, but the others were amazed and marveled (Acts 2:7,12).

Also notice that Peter was able to preach a very

accurate and powerful message (Acts 2:14-40) — something he could not have done if he had been inebriated.

Remember that those who were gathered were devout and God-fearing Jews who would not have listened to Peter if they thought he was drunk. But not only did they listen, many believed what he said and repented. In fact, following Peter's powerful message (which incidentally was filled with meaningful Scriptural content that appealed to reason) 3,000 repented and were baptized (Acts 2:41).

Contrast this event with people who are "drunk in the Spirit" today — who have difficulty testifying about what God has done for them and who often can't speak, walk, or stand. Is this the fruit of the same Spirit who visited these men at Pentecost? Certainly not!

Furthermore, the testimonies that are given today tend to revolve around the experiences rather than around Jesus Christ and Scripture as Peter's sermon did.

Peter answered the mockers, "For these men are not drunk, as you suppose" (Acts 2:15). He added, "but this is what was spoken of through the prophet Joel" (Acts 2:16).

Joel 2:28-32 (which Peter quoted from) states:

> And it will come about after this that I will pour out My Spirit on all mankind; and your sons and daughters will prophesy, your old men will dream dreams, your young men will see visions. And even on the male and female servants I will pour out My Spirit in those days. And I will display wonders in the sky and on the earth, blood, fire, and columns of smoke. The sun will be turned into darkness, and the moon into blood, before the great and awesome day of the Lord comes. And it will come about that whoever calls on the name of the Lord will be delivered ....

While many foolishly say, "Have a drink at Joel's place," Joel does not mention or suggest that drunken behavior is a sign of the outpouring of God's Spirit. Furthermore, there is no example anywhere in the New

Testament of believers being "drunk in the Spirit." In fact, one of the fruits of the Spirit is self-control (Galatians 5:23) while one of the deeds of the flesh is drunkenness (Galatians 5:21).

Consider Ephesians

Ephesians 5:18 says, "And do not get drunk with wine, for that is dissipation, but be filled with the Spirit."

Being filled with the Spirit in this passage does not imply that one will experience some euphoric state of mind resulting in drunken behavior; quite the contrary, it is the antithesis of it. In the context of Ephesians 5, being filled with the Spirit means you are to let the Spirit so totally control you that you will live a life of obedience and discipline. This text in no way gives sanction to drunken-like behavior of the so-called "being drunk in the Spirit" enthusiasts.

The Wine of God's Wrath

"Intoxicating wine" is often used in Scripture to signify God's wrath, but never the outpouring of His Spirit:

• Jeremiah 13:13,14 –

Then say to them, "Thus says the Lord, 'Behold I am about to fill all the inhabitants of this land — the kings that sit for David on his throne, the priests, the prophets and all the inhabitants of Jerusalem — with drunkenness! And I will dash them against each other, both the fathers and the sons together,' declares the Lord. 'I will not show pity nor be sorry nor have compassion that I should not destroy them.' "

• Jeremiah 25:15,16 –

For thus the Lord, the God of Israel, says to me, "Take this cup of the wine of wrath from My hand, and cause all the nations, to whom I send you, to drink it. And they shall drink and stagger and go mad because of the sword that I will send among them."

• Jeremiah 25:27-29 –

And you shall say to them, "Thus says the Lord of hosts, the God of Israel, 'Drink, be drunk, vomit, fall, and rise no more because of the sword which I will send among you.' And it will be, if they refuse to take the cup from your hand to drink, then you will say to them, 'Thus says the Lord of hosts: "You shall surely drink! For behold, I am beginning to work calamity in this city which is called by My name, and shall you be completely free from punishment? You will not be free from punishment; for I am summoning a sword against all the inhabitants of the earth,"' declares the Lord of hosts."

• Jeremiah 51:7 –

Babylon has been a golden cup in the hand of the Lord, intoxicating all the earth. The nations have drunk of her wine; therefore the nations are going mad.

• Psalms 60:3 –

Thou hast made Thy people experience hardship; Thou hast given us wine to drink that makes us stagger.

• Isaiah 51:17 –

Rouse yourself! Rouse yourself! Arise, O Jerusalem, You who have drunk from the Lord's hand the cup of His anger; The chalice of reeling you have drained to the dregs.

• Ezekiel 23:32,33 –

Thus says the Lord God, "You will drink your sister's cup, which is deep and wide. You will be laughed at and held in derision; it contains much. You will be filled with drunkenness and sorrow, the cup of horror and desolation, the cup of your sister Samaria."

• Revelation 14:8 –

And another angel, a second one, followed, saying, "Fallen, fallen is Babylon the great, she who has made all the nations drink of the wine of the passion of her immorality."

• Revelation 17:1,2,6 –

And one of the seven angels who had the seven bowls came and spoke with me, saying, "Come here, I shall show you the judgment of the great harlot who sits on many waters, with whom the kings of the earth committed acts of immorality, and those who dwell on the earth were made drunk with the wine of her immorality." And I saw the woman drunk with the blood of the saints, and with the blood of the witnesses of Jesus ....

Be Sober and on Guard

So the next time you are encouraged or tempted to leave your mind at the door and "belly-on-up to the bar," just remember this: The Spirit of God is the Spirit of truth. In order to receive truth the mind cannot be by-passed. When you release yourself to a mindless, intoxicated state, you are setting yourself up for the product of vain imaginations or demonic delusions. You compromise your God-given responsibility to walk soberly and carefully under the control of His Spirit, His wisdom, and His understanding.

God is a God of order, not chaos. Just look around at His beautiful and majestic creation. There you will see design, order, harmony, and restrained power. Compare this to the chaotic mess of the "drunken and disorderly conduct" of the "drunk-in-the-Spirit" crowd. You be the judge of who is the author of this confusion.

But consider this: Proponents of "holy laughter" and "being drunk in the Spirit" may be right when they say God is the one causing these phenomena to happen. II Thessalonians 2:10,11 indicates that **God will send a strong delusion** upon those who do not love the truth. It is becoming increasingly evident based on the phenomena, "new revelations," and beliefs that so easily have come to be embraced, that they do not have a love for the truth of God's Word!

"Drunk in the Spirit" is definitely not a sign of the outpouring of God's Spirit. But it is fleshly and even sometimes demonic behavior.

What Ever Happened to the Word of God?

Returning to my observations regarding these groups and their bizarre behavior, let me add that it is not uncommon to see people lying flat on the floor as though they were stuck there with glue. In fact they say it is caused by "Holy Ghost glue." Nowhere in Scripture can we find the basis for this bizarre behavior, but being demonically controlled or frozen with fear is commonly manifested in the occult.

Although proponents of "holy laughter" admit that these phenomena are very distracting and make what is being said from the pulpit irrelevant, they believe it is God who is doing the distracting. But I Corinthians 14:33 plainly states, "for God is not a God of confusion but of peace ...." "Confusion" *(akatastasia),* according to Vine's *Expository Dictionary of New Testament Words,* "denotes a state of disorder, disturbance, tumult." I Corinthians 14:40 says, "But let all things be done properly and in an orderly manner."

Proponents of "holy laughter" claim to be receiving a new anointing accompanied by joy and a fresh outpouring of the Holy Spirit. They testify to some of the most powerful services they have ever experienced — changing lives and transforming congregations. Many claim renewed faith, marriages, and ministries.

Those who endorse "holy laughter" and related phenomena seldom give Scripture to support their belief. If any Scripture references are given, they are taken out of context and given a twisted meaning. They give a subjective reason — I experienced it, therefore it must be of God. Resorting to "human wisdom," they set aside the Word of God. Having no Scriptural basis, proponents of "holy laughter" claim that God is doing a new work in His Church that goes beyond the Word of God.

Those drawn to this type of emotionally driven experience very often are discouraged and depressed pastors or Christians who are burnt out and feel powerless in their fruitless ministries. They turn to "holy laughter" and other strange, nonscriptural phenomena and teachings to revitalize their lives and ministries.

I wonder where their relationship was with the Christ of the Scriptures and the fullness of His Spirit, since most claimed to be Spirit-filled before. And because these were obviously lacking, I see why such an inferior experience (when compared to the genuine moving of God's Spirit in Scripture) can so powerfully affect them.

Pastors and believers who seem to be so hungry for the outpouring of God's Spirit are becoming impatient, and thereby are accepting an imitation and counterfeit experience. Many false cult and occult groups started with people who got into false teaching by basing their beliefs on subjective experience rather than the Word of God. This is exactly what is happening to many Christians and pastors today.

For example, Edgar Cayce, who historians falsely recount as a deeply religious Christian, was unsure whether his psychic abilities came from God or the devil. But following his own personal experience, and with the urging of his family and friends, Cayce began doing psychic healings. Also consider, much of the phenomena in Scripture that is often attributed to the demonic (struck dumb and unable to speak, uncontrollable shaking and convulsions, thrown around like a rag doll) is now occurring to Christians and pastors.

Revelation is being fulfilled. The Lord's return draws closer. The "Church," however, laughs uncontrollably, rolls around on the floor in convulsions, and is struck dumb — unable to speak. What a far cry from New Testament Christianity and the power of God's Spirit manifested in the book of Acts.

A couple recently told me about an evangelist who spoke at their church and advertised that there would be signs, wonders, and miracles. I asked this couple to give me examples of signs, wonders, and miracles in the Bible. They gave me an impressive listing. But then I asked, "And what signs, wonders, and miracles actually occurred through this evangelist?" They acknowledged that his were in no way even remotely comparable to the Biblical accounts.

"Peace" is Blissed-Out Meditative Trance

Proponents of "holy laughter" misuse Scripture. Their method of Biblical interpretation is faulty because they take verses out of context. Using their method I could easily take every text dealing with the word "peace" and, by their reasoning, justify the Eastern phenomenon of the "blissed-out meditative trance" and claim it is the work of the Holy Spirit. I could then go around the world conducting "holy peace" crusades and by my "holy" touch zap people into nirvana.

But why stop there? I could take the Scriptural references regarding bodily translation, like Enoch when he was translated into heaven, and Philip when he was translated out of the presence of the Ethiopian eunuch, and have people line up to have hands laid on them to be translated into heaven, another room, or another country.

Read All the Scriptures

I have seen the Scriptures given by "holy laughter" proponents (Job 5:22; 8:21; Psalm 16:11; 37:12,13; 126:1,2; Proverbs 15:13; Nehemiah 8:10; Acts 2:28; 3:19; etc). On the surface they make it appear to be Biblical. But when I checked each passage in context, I realized they have been twisted and taken out of context.

Those who endorse "drunkenness" and "holy laughter" in these last days should also read a few more Scriptures.

Luke 21:34-36 –

> Be on guard, that your hearts may not be weighted down with dissipation and drunkenness and the worries of life, and that day come on you suddenly like a trap; for it will come upon all those who dwell on the face of all the earth. But keep on the alert at all times, praying in order that you may have strength to escape all these things that are about to take place, and to stand before the Son of Man.

Romans 13:12-14 –

> The night is almost gone, and the day is at hand. Let us therefore lay aside the deeds of darkness and put on the armor of light. Let us behave properly as in the day, not in carousing and drunkenness, not in sexual promiscuity and sensuality, not in strife and

jealousy. But put on the Lord Jesus Christ, and make no provision for the flesh in regard to its lusts.

James 4:7-10 –

Submit therefore to God. Resist the devil and he will flee from you. Draw near to God and He will draw near to you. Cleanse your hands, you sinners; and purify your hearts, you double-minded. Be miserable and mourn and weep; let your laughter be turned into mourning, and your joy to gloom. Humble yourselves in the presence of the Lord, and He will exalt you.

I Peter 4:7 –

The end of all things is at hand; therefore, be of sound judgment and sober spirit for the purpose of prayer.

I Peter 5:8 –

Be of sober spirit, be on the alert. Your adversary, the devil, prowls about like a roaring lion, seeking someone to devour.

Jeremiah 12:8 –

My inheritance has become to Me like a lion in the forest; she has roared against Me; therefore I have come to hate her.

Jeremiah 51:37-39 (NIV) –

"Babylon will be a heap of ruins, a haunt of jackals, an object of horror and scorn, a place where no one lives. Her people all roar like young lions, they growl like lion cubs. But while they are aroused, I will set out a feast for them and make them drunk, so that they shout with laughter — then sleep forever and not awake," declares the Lord.

Lay Hands on No Man Suddenly

I Timothy 5:22 states, "Lay hands suddenly on no man, neither be partaker of other men's sins: keep thyself pure" (KJV). So too, we must be cautious whom we permit to lay hands on us. Once you go up front for an evangelist, prophet, or apostle to pray for you, you have submitted to them. You are now vulnerable to be influenced by their power. If they are propagating nonbiblical beliefs or techniques, or demonic powers, that could be as potentially dangerous as submitting to someone in an occult meeting.

I believe that Christians who are submitting to "slain in the Spirit," "holy laughter," and other unbiblical, oftentimes occultic phenomena are in the same spiritual danger as those who attend seances or play with ouija boards. In the months and years to come they will experience the same physical, mental, emotional, and spiritual oppression that those who dabble in the occult eventually do.

It is also interesting that the same spirit I encountered through spiritual warfare and confronting witches, spiritualists, mediums, satanists, and New Agers for twenty years is now manifest in the Church.

Resembles Hindu Occultism to Me

The phenomena of "slain in the Spirit" and "holy laughter" are about as impressive and about as Scriptural as Guru Maharaj Ji's techniques which supposedly enabled his adherents to see the "Divine light of God," hear the "Divine music of God," feel the "Word of God in their flesh," and taste the "Divine nectar of God."

According to researcher Ellis Stewart's article on *Hindu Occultism:*

> The most feared and revered deity in Hinduism is the goddess Kali (Durga), the wife of Shiva the destroyer. She is also known as Shakti, which means 'force', and represents the impersonal force that occultism teaches runs the universe. The divine power-touch of the guru is called shaktipat. This is a term used for the touch (or near touch) of a guru's hand to the worshipper's forehead that produces supernatural effects. Shakti literally means power; and in administering the shaktipat the guru becomes a channel of primal power, the cosmic power (so they believe) underlying the universe. The supernatural effect of shakti through the guru's touch may knock the worshiper to the floor or he may see a bright light and receive an experience of enlightenment or inner illumination, or have some other mystical or psychic experience.[18]

Pastor Catapulted From Chair

A magazine article by proponents of "holy laughter" boasted of a pastor, who while quietly weeping and worshiping, was suddenly catapulted from his chair. He flew through the air nearly ten feet down the aisle, landing on his face. This does not even remotely resemble the Holy Spirit in the Bible, but it does resemble demonic manifestations in the occult.

While talking to some leaders endorsing the "Toronto blessing," I asked, "How far can this phenomena go before you say 'enough is enough'?" One of them immediately responded, "You're being judgmental. This conversation is terminated!" I said, "I'm not being judgmental. I'm just trying to find a Biblical basis for your endorsement of this supposed 'outpouring of God's Spirit.' " But they refused to even discuss it.

On another occasion a friend of ours, who attends a charismatic church, was physically escorted out of the church because he questioned the pastor concerning the Scriptural basis of his teaching. There are also many prophecies and pronouncements of destruction on those who oppose — and sometimes on those who merely don't go along with their teachings and practices.

It's Nowhere to be Found in Scripture

It is a sad day when those for whom Christ died, and for whom He wants to return to take as His own Bride to be with Him for eternity, are so far removed from true Biblical Christianity that they are becoming in a sense spiritual prostitutes. Once I dreamed the Lord was speaking through me to a group of people who were embracing false teaching. I said to them: "How diabolical that something ['holy laughter'] which is not even in Scripture is causing so many church splits, divisions, and turmoil in the body of Christ!" Historically, most heresies and divisions in the church have at least started with some aspect of Scripture. But this error has absolutely no basis in God's Word, and yet it is dividing the church. It illustrates how far removed people are from a knowledge of true Biblical Christianity.

There are Christians who choose to embrace their own subjective personal experiences rather than the objective, inspired Word of God. Consequently, they are involving themselves in so-called "manifestations of the Holy Spirit" which are becoming more and more bizarre and visibly demonic ("the cup of demons," I Corinthians 10:21, not the "new wine of the Holy Spirit"). Some of their behavior is "sexual immorality around the altar." Unless they repent they will soon suffer the consequences as they find the Lord "making war against them" (Revelation 2:16).

God sent Judah into Babylonian captivity because the people and leaders would not respond to His discipline and set up abominable idols in the house that bears His name and defiled it (Jeremiah 32:32-34). Far worse today is that believers and leaders have defiled the Church by participating in occultic techniques around the very altar of God, not to mention the demonic manifestations occurring in individual believers, temples of the Holy Spirit.

"Close Encounters" at Toronto Airport

A missionary couple I met while ministering in Haiti had attended the Toronto Airport Vineyard (now Toronto Airport Christian Fellowship) when the phenomena first began to manifest. They told me they were greatly confused by the unscriptural phenomena, but were unable to voice their opinion lest they be considered unspiritual. When I asked them if they felt the phenomena going on there was of God, the flesh, or demonic, they quickly replied, "Much of it was demonic!"

A team of us (some who were raised in and attend Pentecostal and charismatic churches) visited the Toronto church and saw not only uncontrollable laughter and weeping, but also people "drunk in the Spirit," struck dumb, and stuck like glue. We witnessed people doing every imaginable contortion, twitching, and jerking movement. Many of them fell backwards in ecstatic trances or their bodies shook violently out of control. While the speaker was trying to preach, we heard gut-wrenching groaning, shrieking, warrior cries, animal noises, and a garbled "prophecy" by a pastor's wife who was acting like a wild woman shaking, jerking, and swirling her head around in quick spasmodic motions. Parts of the service resembled a voodoo ritual, people on drugs, or a psychiatric ward more than a Spirit-filled service. To think that tens of thousands of people and pastors had visited this place — many to take the "Toronto blessing" back to their churches!

When I returned from Toronto, my Bible study just happened to appropriately include II Timothy 4:1-5 which says:

> I solemnly charge you in the presence of God and of Christ Jesus, who is to judge the living and the dead, and by His appearing and His kingdom: preach the word; be ready in season and out of season; reprove, rebuke, exhort, with great patience and instruction. For the time will come when they will not endure sound doctrine; but wanting to have their ears tickled, they will accumulate for themselves teachers in accordance to their own desires; and will turn away their ears from the truth, and will turn aside to myths. But you, be sober in all things ....

Reflects the Occult More Than the Scriptural Norm

Many claim that various phenomena such as falling down, laughing, shaking, jerking, jumping up and down, feelings of warmth and electricity, and other such experiences occur when the Holy Spirit comes on a person. These sensations and behavior far more resemble the occult and self-induced experience than they represent the norm in Scripture of God's Spirit moving in a person's life.

The Holy Spirit "isn't energy or electricity or anything that any human being can pump, scoop, blow, charge with, or press into another person. The Holy Spirit is

God. Even when we speak of the 'power' of the Holy Spirit, this is not some energy .... [Energy] is a New Age concept, not a Biblical one." [19]

The desire to turn off the mind, lose control of oneself, and have euphoric experiences are primary characteristics of occultism and Eastern mysticism — not Biblical Christianity. For example, in an issue of SCP Newsletter, a quote was included from the book, *The Stormy Search for the Self*, in which New Age authors, Christina and Stanislav Grof, state:

> During powerful rushes of Kundalini energy, [individuals] often emit various involuntary sounds, and their bodies move in strange and unexpected patterns. Among the most common manifestations ... are unmotivated and unnatural laughter or crying ... and imitating a variety of animal sounds and movements.[20]

You might say, "The atmosphere was positive and very exciting, and everyone seemed warm and friendly. I felt great and so close to the Lord that it had to be the Holy Spirit." Well, I've been in many occult and New Age meetings and believe me, they are very positive, there is electricity in the air, and there is a great excitement and expectancy of what "God" is going to do.

The former Oregon guru, Bhagwhan Shree Rajneesh, was often referred to as being "drunk on the divine." He would draw his followers to himself and ask them to "drink" from him. His spiritual "wine" could be gotten by merely a touch of his hand to the head. After his touch many would fall to the floor in ecstasy.[21]

The Indian saint, Ramakrishna, would daily go into "samadhi," a trance-like stupor "in which one involuntarily falls down unconscious and enters a rapturous state of super-conscious bliss (ananda) .... These states could last anywhere from a few minutes to several days and were often accompanied by uncontrollable laughter or weeping. He could send others into this state with a single touch to the head or chest."[22]

Swami Baba Muktananda, through what his followers

called shaktipat (physical touch), would transfer "guru's grace" to his followers, triggering the awakening of the Kundalini, producing "uncontrollable laughing, roaring, barking, hissing, crying, shaking, etc. Some devotees became mute or unconscious. Many felt themselves being infused with feelings of great joy and peace and love."[23]

We can see by these examples that it is often the case that false religious experiences are manifested by warm feelings and great joy. During the 1960s and '70s, the massive influence of Eastern religions and occult practices drew the Western world into a feelings-oriented frenzy. Devotees rejected the cold orthodoxy of the established church for the more subjective emotional experience of Eastern religions. No longer was validation based on the external, objective Word of God, but rather on internal, subjective impulses. Reason was cast aside like some tattered old tool. The cultural cry of that age, "If it feels good — do it," penetrated the Church. But how you *feel* can never be the ultimate criterion for evaluating phenomena and experiences. Proper interpretation of Scripture, or in other words, rightly dividing the Word of Truth, is where we must begin in determining how we walk in this world until Christ returns.

I'm Not Impressed by Phenomena...

"Slain in the Spirit," "holy laughter," and so-called miracles, healings, prophecies, and revelations by themselves do not impress me. I have seen them occur in various cult, occult, Eastern mystical, and New Age groups which I have researched.

Many Christians go to a meeting, and because the Bible is used or the name of Jesus is mentioned, they ignorantly accept everything that happens as being from God. Yet, I have researched seances and spiritualist meetings and attended many occult and New Age gatherings where they quoted the Bible, talked about Jesus and even raised their hands to supposedly praise Him. Some actually professed to be Spirit-filled

Christians living under His Lordship. Many Hindu gurus and practitioners of black magic and occultism use both Scripture and the name of Jesus to validate their unscriptural beliefs and practices.

Bring on the Fortune-Tellers and Mediums

I'm convinced that in many Christian circles mediums and fortune-tellers could come in, and if they prayed in Jesus' name, or raised their hands to praise Jesus or quoted a few Scriptures and then operated their fortune-telling and their mediumistic gifts, most in attendance wouldn't even know the difference and would believe it was the Holy Spirit.

Johanna Michaelsen believes in the gifts of the Holy Spirit. In her book, *The Beautiful Side of Evil,* she warns believers to discern the gifts because, as she says, "We shouldn't be too surprised to find practicing occultists within most of our denominations ...."

She goes on to say:

> For example, believers with occultic backgrounds which have never been renounced are manifesting mediumistic gifts and techniques which go undiscerned in the atmosphere of ecstatic hoopla which frequently characterizes so many meetings ....

> Mediumistic gifts can, but do not always, automatically disappear when one becomes a believer. Mine didn't. I was more psychic than ever ... and from what I've seen in many of our meetings, my abilities would have been acclaimed as the gift of 'words of knowledge' and 'prophecy.' It was actually clairvoyance.

> It was not until I took the *offensive* in my ongoing battle against Satan, making a *full* list of *all* my sins ... renouncing them and all the works and gifts of Satan, and then *totally* refraining from practicing these things, that these psychic powers faded over a period of months. It has been so with many others whom I've counseled. I truly believe that those with occultic backgrounds should wait a season before seeking and exercising any of the more spectacular gifts of the Spirit until they have matured in the grace and knowledge of the Lord.[24]

The Occult Connection

I went to a meeting to hear a female evangelist who supposedly operated in all the gifts of the Holy Spirit. But after hearing her, I was convinced she was either operating in the flesh or by a demonic spirit, but definitely not by the Spirit of God.

You would be surprised how all these alleged born again, Spirit-filled Christians would run up front to be "slain in the Spirit," to have hands laid on them for healing, and to be prophesied over. They played her tapes over and over before going to bed, so they could listen to every word that she had from the Lord for them. But as I talked to these Christians, I was appalled at their immaturity, their ignorance of God's Word, and their lack of discernment.

The female evangelist, whom they practically worshiped, gave several false prophecies and many unimpressive "miracles." She called forward an older lady and told her the reason she always had a sad face was because she had a glandular problem. Before praying for her, she assured her that she would go back to her seat healed and with a smile. Again she was wrong, as the sad-faced lady went back to her seat unchanged. Later I learned that her saddened condition was due to the recent deaths of her husband and son and was not caused by a glandular problem.

It seemed that no matter what problem anyone had, her solution was for them to go forward, receive a few words of prophecy and a prayer for healing, be "slain in the Spirit," and everything would be okay — but it wasn't. I knew in my spirit that this evangelist had been involved in the occult before supposedly becoming a Christian. The same false prophecies, the same Scripture-twisting, and the same spiritual warfare I had encountered while interviewing, researching, and witnessing to fortune-tellers and mediums, I experienced in dealing with this evangelist.

I told my research director that if I could get a taped interview with her (something she had refused to do), I could prove that somewhere in her past there was an occult connection. Even though several people had finally realized what I was saying was true and left her group, no one was able or willing to show me the "occult connection" in her background.

Finally, after several years of tremendous opposition from members of this group, a woman who heard me on the radio called and said, "I can confirm something for you. I know a former neighbor of this lady, and she was, in fact, a fortune-teller before." I said, "That's what the Holy Spirit has been showing me for years. That's what I knew from God's Word and Spirit, and my research, and now you're finally confirming it." She nevertheless continued to operate her fortune-telling gift under the guise of Christianity — duping her foolish followers.

Discerning Demonic Counterfeits

A woman called me concerning help for a man she knew. During our conversation, she began to speak in tongues to impress me with the fact that she had been filled with the Spirit. But I discerned her tongues to be counterfeit. She told me she was baptized in the Spirit. I said, "You must really be hungry for God's Word and reading it every day." She said, "Oh, no! I don't have time or the need to read it anymore. Jesus often appears and speaks directly to me now."

I am seeing an increasing "demonic connection" as more and more supposed Christians are either experiencing or manifesting demonic phenomena. Just as there are tragic consequences for those who become involved in the occult — physically, mentally, emotionally, and spiritually — so too, I am seeing a pattern of resulting tragedies manifest in the lives of many "Christians" who are ignorantly or purposely becoming involved in occult and New Age techniques, practices, and beliefs being taught in their churches.

Much of what is being said and written today seems good on the surface, sounds Scriptural, and seems to exalt Jesus. We must remember, however, the following Scriptural accounts:

1) In Luke 4:34, a demon-possessed man cried out to

Jesus, "I know who You are — the Holy One of God!"

2) During his temptation of Jesus, recorded in Matthew 4:1-11, Satan quoted Scripture, but subtly twisted its meaning.

3) In Acts 16:16-18, we read an account of a slave-girl who had a spirit of divination. She followed after Paul and kept crying out, "These men are bond-servants of the Most High God, who are proclaiming to you the way of salvation." Paul's response was to cast the spirit out.

II Kings states:

> They worshiped the Lord, but they also served their own gods in accordance with the customs of the nations from which they had been brought. Even while these people were worshiping the Lord, they were serving their idols. To this day their children and grandchildren continue to do as their fathers did (17:33,41- NIV).

The Spirit of Simon the Sorcerer

Many today are seeking to use the Holy Spirit for spiritual power and personal advancement.

Acts 8:18-22 records:

> Now when Simon [the Sorcerer] saw that the Spirit was bestowed through the laying on of the apostles' hands, he offered them money, saying, "Give this authority to me as well, so that everyone on whom I lay my hands may receive the Holy Spirit." But Peter said to him, "May your silver perish with you, because you thought you could obtain the gift of God with money! You have no part or portion in this matter, for your heart is not right before God. Therefore repent of this wickedness of yours, and pray the Lord that if possible, the intention of your heart may be forgiven you."

The same spirit of Simon is manifest in many believers and Christian leaders today as they are seeking power to perform signs and wonders, not just to advance the Gospel, but for their own ulterior motives.

While Peter would not offer the gift of the Holy Spirit for financial gain, many supposed Christian leaders are more than willing to "sell" Him to gullible followers.

The False Prophet Deceives the World With "Miracles"

How does the False Prophet deceive those who dwell on the earth? Revelation 13:14 answers:

And he deceives those who dwell on the earth because of the signs which it was given him to perform in the presence of the beast [Antichrist], telling those who dwell on the earth to make an image to the beast who had the wound of the sword and has come to life.

Revelation 13:13 says:

And he performs great signs, so that he even makes fire come down out of heaven to the earth in the presence of men.

Paul tells us about this in II Thessalonians 2:8,9:

And then that lawless one will be revealed whom the Lord will slay with the breath of His mouth and bring to an end by the appearance of His coming; that is, the one whose coming is in accord with the activity of Satan, with all power and signs and false wonders.

Revelation 16:13,14 states:

And I saw coming out of the mouth of the dragon and out of the mouth of the beast and out of the mouth of the false prophet, three unclean spirits like frogs; for they are spirits of demons, performing signs, which go out to the kings of the whole world, to gather them together for the war of the great day of God, the Almighty.

Revelations 19:20 says:

And the beast was seized, and with him the false prophet who performed the signs in his presence, by which he deceived those who had received the mark of the beast and those who worshiped his image; these two were thrown alive into the lake of fire which burns with brimstone.

We are living in a day of great deception, and Scripture strongly indicates it is going to accelerate. I am convinced that many Christians who live by the experiential, who follow signs and wonders, who lack discernment, and who don't rightly divide the Word of

Truth are being deceived by the great delusion Paul prophesied would overtake those who reject a love for the truth (II Thessalonians 2:10). And if so many are being deceived now, how do they expect to stand when the deception gets even more difficult to discern as the very incarnation of Satan comes on the scene, and numerous amazing false miracles, signs, and wonders occur?

A Sobering Warning From Christ

Jesus says in Matthew 7:20, "… you will know them by their fruits" — not by their gifts or power or miracles. Satan can counterfeit the gifts of the Spirit, but he can't duplicate the genuine fruit of the Spirit.

Jesus went on in Matthew 7:21-23 to give one of the most startling concepts in Scripture:

> Not everyone who says to Me, "Lord, Lord," will enter the kingdom of heaven; but he who does the will of My Father who is in heaven. Many will say to Me on that day, "Lord, Lord, did we not prophesy in Your name, and in Your name cast out demons, and in Your name perform many miracles?" And then I will declare to them, "I never knew you; Depart from Me, you who practice lawlessness."

These people used Biblical terminology. They called Him Lord. They supposedly prophesied in His name, performed miracles in His name, and cast out demons in His name, but that is not the validation. As much as we need the gifts of the Spirit in our lives and ministries, that is not the criterion for receiving His approval.

Jesus will not say, "I knew you because you prophesied in My name," "because you cast out demons in My name," or "because you did miracles in My name." No! If that's the basis of why you think He should let you into His kingdom, then He will say to you, "Depart from Me, I never knew you."

The requirement is knowing Him personally and, "He who does the will of My Father who is in heaven." That's why I am not impressed by the phenomena that go on. What is really important is that you *know* the Jesus of the Bible in a real and intimate way, that He is *truly* Lord of your life, that you are walking in obedience to His Word and Spirit, that you are being conformed to His image, that your heart's desire is to exalt and glorify Him, that you are bearing fruit for His glory, and the fruit of the Spirit is being manifested in your life!

Former "Head-hunters" Seek the Real Thing

I ministered at a national convention in the Himalayan Mountains in India to people coming out of backgrounds of Hinduism, Buddhism, idolatry, spiritism, ancestor worship, demon worship, sorcery, witchcraft, and various other forms of occultism and mysticism. These people, some of whom were former witch-doctors and "head-hunters," did not want to be influenced by mere hype, emotionalism, and imitations of the Holy Spirit — or by any counterfeit techniques.

In some of the mountain villages, many of these people pay a great price to live for Christ. They are forsaken by families and friends and are stoned and beaten with bamboo sticks for witnessing and speaking about Christ. Before I spoke I was told that these people would evaluate everything I said by Scripture — and it had better be accurate. When I spoke God greatly honored His Word. After every message, hundreds came to the altar where God moved on hearts in a powerful way.

It is ironic to me that so many Christians are settling for inferior and counterfeit experiences and are involving themselves in the beliefs, practices, and techniques that these people renounced when they came to Christ. Many of these people who have come out of a background of mysticism and occultism are seeking to live a New Testament Christianity, and are seeing God move in such a powerful way.

I Refuse to Settle for Less Than the Genuine

There are three main problems with the current trends and phenomena in experience-driven Christianity. First, they are unsupported by God's Word. Second, they are found flourishing in the occult, Eastern mysticism, and the New Age movement. And third, the phenomena and "miracles" are blatantly inferior to that which is recorded in Scripture.

I want everything God has, but I refuse to settle for an imitation or a counterfeit. However, before I can receive the genuine, I have to be honest. The power does not come from me, nor do I control when or how it operates. I can't tolerate gimmickry. I can't use New Age techniques, mind control, or mass hypnosis. I can't camouflage the "power of ki/ch'i" (impersonal energy force) as the Holy Spirit. I can't try to pass off a "spirit guide" as the Holy Spirit. I can't pass on emotion and hype and say, "That's the Holy Spirit." I can't push on your head and knock you down or work you into an emotional frenzy and exclaim, "See how God's Spirit is moving!" I can't use psychosomatic healing techniques and claim that it is God's supernatural power.

The Lord is calling the body of Christ to integrity! We cannot hide behind a smoke screen of superficial spirituality.

I will not settle for anything less than the genuine moving of the Holy Spirit. And that is why I'm seeking Him so strongly.

From my research into the last days, the New Age movement, the current trends infiltrating the Church, and from my study of God's Word and the witness of His Spirit through many hours of prayer and fasting, I am convinced that we are in the midst of the prophesied apostasy and deception. I also believe we are on the verge of a genuine outpouring of and empowering by God's Spirit before Christ's Second Coming. That is why Satan is raising up so much imitation and counterfeit. I believe those who stay faithful to the Jesus of the Bible and the Word of God will be supernaturally empowered by His Spirit. In the midst of persecution we will see the resurrection power of Christ as manifested in the book of Acts and in the prophesies of Joel 2 — as well as an increase of the imitation and counterfeit.

That's why I'm saying, "Beware; be alert!" That's why

I challenge you to seek to know the Word of God, and to develop discernment and a sensitivity to God's Spirit through prayer and fasting.

We will not witness the genuine outpouring of His Spirit if we tolerate gimmickry, manifestations of flesh, and counterfeits, or if we accept any other technique or practice, attempting to deceive ourselves or others into believing it is the Holy Spirit.

When the genuine Spirit of Christ comes upon you, He doesn't make you fall over, stagger, act like a drunk, be struck dumb, or manifest other bizarre and useless displays of "power." No! When the Spirit of God empowers you, He gives you faith, confidence, courage, boldness, strength, power, peace, joy, love, self-control, wisdom, and all that is needed to share the Gospel, live a godly life, and accomplish that which He has called you to do!

Seek His Will

One thing I know for certain is that I cannot initiate or attempt to force His supernatural manifestation, but I must seek His will, totally submit to Him, and rely on His sovereign intervention in His time and His way.

Those who seek the Lord daily with their whole heart through His Word, prayer, and fasting will *know* Him. They will not settle for imitation, counterfeit, and inferior power, signs, and wonders, for they will walk in discernment, and the *true* power of the resurrected Christ will be manifested in their lives. Initially their power might not seem as impressive, but in the end it will prove far superior, for it is derived from the one true God, His son, Jesus Christ, and the transforming work of His Holy Spirit.

True revival and the outpouring of God's Spirit is not the result of man's manipulation or leaders showing off their supposed power and gifts. It is God's sovereign intervention in response to those who in humility and brokenness seek the Lord with all their hearts.

True revival will come when we hunger and thirst for the Jesus of the Bible, as a drowning man desires a breath of fresh air. When we do, we will seek His Word, pray and fast, and clean up our lives. As committed Christians we need to use discernment, stay true to God's Word, maintain a testimony for the Jesus of the Bible, and walk in the *genuine power* of His Spirit!

Apostasy Now! –
Coming Soon to a Church Near You

As I watched several "Christian" television programs, I witnessed subtle and blatant Scripture-twisting as well as unbiblical phenomena. I was grieved in my spirit and said to my wife, "It's as though we are seeing right before our eyes the apostate church and whore of Babylon that will help bring about the temporary reign of the Antichrist."

Through this book and in many other ways, I have been exposing the deception going on in the body of Christ. For years I received "black eyes" in many Christian circles for speaking out, but with all the obvious deception, fakery, greed, and immorality now occurring, many are realizing why I have been warning so strongly! What we are seeing is just the tip of the iceberg. God is exposing many who are merchandising the Gospel, living in immorality, and using deceit and deception. Only those walking before Him in truth and integrity will be standing when it's all over!

As religious shysters are exposed, Christians will have their eyes opened. Monies that once were sent to false ministries will now, hopefully, be given to genuine ministries and churches. These funds can then be used to help get the true Gospel of Jesus Christ to all the world before our Lord's return, instead of being used to build someone's personal bank account and estate.

Jude 3-7

In light of increasing deception in the Church, let's examine several timely verses in the book of Jude.

[On the following pages, Scripture is printed in bold and the italic comments in brackets are mine.]

Jude 3-7 states:

Dear friends, although I was very eager to write to you about the salvation we share,

[I, too, would much rather only write about our salvation in Christ.]

I felt I had to write and urge you to contend for the faith that was once for all entrusted to the saints.

[We are living in a day and age when we must boldly stand for the faith — the truth of Biblical Christianity not some "new revelation" or the distorted Gospel of today.]

For certain men whose condemnation was written about long ago have secretly slipped in among you. They are godless men, who change the grace of our God into a license for immorality and deny Jesus Christ our only Sovereign and Lord.

[They appear to be apostles and prophets of Christ, but in reality they are ravenous wolves who are controlled by the lusts of the flesh rather than the fruit of the Spirit. They may profess with their mouth Christ is Lord and even praise and worship Him with their lips, but their true self-centered motives and lifestyle and their Scripture-twisting deny Him as Lord in their hearts.]

Though you already know all this, I want to remind you that the Lord delivered His people out of Egypt, but later destroyed those who did not believe. And the angels who did not keep their positions of authority but abandoned their own home — these He has kept in darkness, bound with everlasting chains for judgment on the great Day. In a similar way, Sodom and Gomorrah and the surrounding towns gave themselves up to sexual immorality and perversion. They serve as an example of those who suffer the punishment of eternal fire.

[God's judgment will eventually fall on those who are

resorting to deceit and deception and who are propagating heresy and the very spirit of antichrist in the Church today.]

Jude 8,9

Jude 8 and 9 continues:

In the very same way, these dreamers pollute their own bodies, reject authority and slander celestial beings.

[They are dreamers because all their unbiblical revelations keep them out of touch with the truth and reality of God's Word. They pollute their bodies with all their greed and immorality. They reject authority by refusing to let anyone in the body of Christ correct them. Some are so arrogant they can be seen on TV ranting and raving against Satan and supposedly stomping him under their feet.]

But even the archangel Michael, when he was disputing with the devil about the body of Moses, did not dare to bring a slanderous accusation against him, but said, "The Lord rebuke you!"

Jude 10-13

Jude 10-13 goes on to say concerning them:

Yet these men speak abusively against whatever they do not understand; and what things they do understand by instinct, like unreasoning animals — these are the very things that destroy them.

Woe to them! They have taken the way of Cain;

[Just as Cain killed Abel, so these false teachers poison others by offering them a tainted Gospel.]

they have rushed for profit into Balaam's error;

[Just as Balaam was motivated by greed and personal gain to seduce the children of Israel from pure devotion to the Lord, so these false teachers today seduce many from pure devotion to Christ.]

they have been destroyed in Korah's rebellion.

[Just as Korah was destroyed for his rebellion before the Lord, the days of these false teachers and false prophets are numbered. They will ultimately be exposed and destroyed.]

These men are blemishes at your love feasts,

[They fulfill the lusts of the flesh and the cravings of their

bellies more than hungering and thirsting for the Lord.]

**eating with you without the slightest qualm —
shepherds who feed only themselves.**

*[Instead of feeding their flock the true Word of God, they
are merely merchandising the Gospel to feed their own
fleshly desires.]*

**They are clouds without rain, blown along by the
wind;**

*[Just as clouds without rain deceive a parched land into
thinking it will get life-giving moisture, so too, these false
teachers deceive their followers into thinking they are
giving them the genuine Bread from Heaven. They are
blown from one new trend or teaching to the next.]*

**autumn trees, without fruit and uprooted — twice
dead. They are wild waves of the sea, foaming up
their shame;**

*[God exposes the true motives of these false teachers just
as the waves turn up much debris from the ocean floor and
leave it lying on the beach for all to see. Their motivation is
not ministry, but prosperity, power, and pleasure.]*

**wandering stars, for whom blackest darkness has
been reserved forever.**

*[Shooting like meteorites across the sky, they come on the
scene and rapidly rise to prominence with their "new
revelations" and phenomena, but their glory is usually
short-lived. Their eternal destiny is terrifying because
they did not heed the Scriptural warning that teachers
will be judged more strictly — James 3:1.]*

Jude 17-20

Jude 17-20 concludes:

**But, dear friends, remember what the apostles of
our Lord Jesus Christ foretold. They said to you,
"In the last times there will be scoffers who will
follow their own ungodly desires." These are the
men who divide you,**

*[It's the false teachers who are tickling the ears of their
listeners with false doctrine, rather than giving them sound
teaching, who are causing the division, not those who are
boldly standing for the truth and exposing the error.]*

**who follow mere natural instincts and do not have
the Spirit.**

[They claim to be the spiritual elite, but they don't even have the Holy Spirit — having a form of godliness but denying its power.]

But you, dear friends, build yourselves up in your most holy faith and pray in the Holy Spirit.

[The truth is proclaimed in God's Word, not all these unbiblical and extra-biblical teachings and revelations. Pray that you may be able to walk in discernment in these last days and in the genuine power of God's Spirit.]

What We Need Today

We need Christian leaders today who will not merchandise the Gospel, but will sacrifice for the sake of the Gospel the way our Lord and His disciples did. We need those who will not resort to hype, mass hysteria, and mind control, or use deceit and deception, but will walk in integrity and the genuine power of the Holy Spirit. We need those who will not tickle the ears of the people with false teaching or proclaim false prophecies or supposed new revelations which are in reality from their own inspiration or from "another spirit."

We need those who will "rightly divide the Word of Truth" and proclaim the pure Word of God under the true anointing of God's Spirit. We need those who will not settle for superficial, inferior, imitation, and counterfeit techniques and phenomena.

There is so much in God's Word that we barely scratch its surface. We need to get into the Scriptures and allow God's Spirit to give us insight. To those who earnestly seek His face and diligently study the Holy Scriptures, He promises to reveal the deep riches of His Word!

A Special Challenge to the
Body of Christ!

We are seeing a famine for the Word of God in our generation. A prophet of old had words to say about this very thing. Amos 8:11,12 warns:

"Behold, days are coming," declares the Lord God, "When I will send a famine on the land, not a famine for bread or a thirst for water, but rather for hearing the words of the Lord. And people will stagger from sea to sea, and from the north even to the east; they will go to and fro to seek the word of the Lord, but they will not find it."

Kids eat all the junk food they can get, because it tastes so good. They live in the "now," so they don't bother to be concerned about the resulting consequences of malnutrition and susceptibility to other adverse consequences such as stomachaches, rotten teeth, and obesity.

Many Christians are doing the same by living on a junk food diet spiritually. All they want is the excitement and blessing without the responsibility, commitment, and discipline. As a result, they are spiritually malnourished and susceptible to false doctrine.

I am shocked by the lack of knowledge of the Word and the lack of discernment manifested by those "Christian" leaders who are propagating these false beliefs and practices I have been exposing, not to mention that of their listeners.

I heard someone say the following about one of these teachers who, I think, is very extreme and unbiblical. They said, "I listened hour after hour for over fifty hours to this person's tapes and I was so full of God's Word that I was just exploding." I thought to myself, "All you got filled with was that person's 'interpretation' of God's Word."

As much as I hope you'll read my books and listen to my tapes, do so with an open Bible. Do not let my words be the foundation of your spiritual diet. Spend more time in God's Word. Far more important than anything I say or anyone else says is your getting into the Word of God and seeking the Lord with all of your heart.

If this person would have spent those fifty hours in God's Word, he would have been much better off. Many hold these teachers and prophets in higher esteem than they hold Jesus Christ, and listen to their tapes and read their books more than they study the Bible — and this should not be so.

Zen Koan

There is a thing in Zen Buddhism called a koan. A koan is a paradox or insoluble problem that you meditate on with the intent to derail your rational mind. It works on the principle that a sudden impasse or jolt to the intellect can bring insight.

I believe that many Christian leaders are doing a Zen koan move on believers without realizing it. Their double talk, their Scripture-twisting, their taking it out of context derails one's rational thinking. Sometimes after I read or listened to one of their teachings, I thought, "Maybe it is Scriptural," until I looked up each verse. It's tedious to do, but when I examined each verse in context, I realized that the Scriptures had been twisted.

Develop Sensitivity and Awareness

Through my martial arts training (before the Lord led me out), I had learned to develop my peripheral vision.

When sparring I could focus on my opponent's eyes or chest area while simultaneously being able to see his hands and feet. This prepared me for whatever attack he might use. I demonstrated this skill when I would go into schools to speak and do self-defense clinics. Looking at students in the center of the audience, I could tell them what other students were doing on both sides.

Many martial artists develop this type of sensitivity and awareness to the degree that they can sense or anticipate their opponent's attack as soon as it begins, and thereby effectively counter the attack. Some go even further. They try to become super sensitive through meditation and by developing the power of ki or ch'i. Their goal is to be able to think their opponent's thoughts and know his moves before he even begins the attack.

If they attempt to develop this much sensitivity to defeat an opponent, how much more should we develop a sensitivity and discernment in submission to God, so He can guide and direct our lives through His Word and Spirit? The benefit of their occultic discernment is only temporary, while the implications of Biblical discernment are eternal.

Seek to be an Expert on God's Word

The responsibility of every Christian is to seek to be an expert on the Word of God. Don't be too quick to accept every new teaching or technique, but examine all teachings, prophecies, revelations, and practices by the Word of God. Then when someone takes verses out of context, adds to, subtracts from, misinterprets, or twists and distorts the Word in order to make it conform to their own idea, you can examine the Scriptures in context and also apply other Scriptures that may give additional light on the subject, thereby rightly dividing the Word of Truth.

The pastor of an exciting and Biblically balanced charismatic church in Minnesota, shared with me the following when I ministered there:

One day in my quiet time the Lord challenged me to

write down my six favorite verses, the ones I could quote by heart. I wrote down Mark 11:24; Philippians 4:13; 4:19; James 4:7; Hebrews 11:1; I Corinthians 1:27. After finishing I felt quite good about it. Then He challenged me to write down the subject and context of those verses. To my surprise I could not do it. When I looked them up I found that their meaning in context was entirely different than I had thought.

Right then I determined to always know the context of a verse before I use it. That simple idea has revolutionized my thinking and ministry. You see, I thought the Church was in the midst of a "Word movement," and realized that it was only in the midst of a "verse movement."

A man writing to me from Australia concerning these "new" teachings and phenomena accurately stated: "When you take the *text* out of *context* you are left with *con* — and that is what is happening in our churches today."

There's a generation of so-called prophets and apostles and false teachers rising up today who are not allowing us to be Berean Christians (Acts 17:10-12). They would have us believe that they are above questioning or correction. But I say, "Be a Berean Christian. Evaluate everything said and done in light of God's Word, and if it's not accurate, then reject it!"

Examine everything that comes into your mind whether it is from radio, television, something you read, or from the pulpit. Make certain it is in accord with the Word of God. Let the Word of God — not your experience; let the Word of God — not evangelists, teachers, prophets, and apostles; let the Word of God — not someone's tapes and books — be your foundation.

Joshua was commanded by God to:

Be strong and very courageous; be careful to do according to all the law which Moses My servant commanded you; do not turn from it to the right or to the left, so that you may have success wherever you go. This book of the law shall not depart from your mouth, but you shall meditate on it day and night, so that you may be careful to do according to all that is written in it; for then you will make your way prosperous, and then you will have success (Joshua 1:7,8).

How much more should we totally build our life on God's Word without turning to the right or to the left to follow extra-biblical and unbiblical revelations and experiences.

George O. Wood states:

> I visited in Rome the prison from which Paul is believed to have written II Timothy prior to his own execution by Caesar. He would have been lowered into the cell through a hole in the ceiling. In the cold dampness of that dimly lit cell, his words brilliantly reach us today and illuminate our hearts. He closes the letter with a charge to Timothy and all Christian leaders: "PREACH THE WORD" (II Timothy 4:2)! He does not say, "Preach your own experience. Preach fads. Preach minor things as major things." No! He says: "PREACH THE WORD!" Why does he say that? Because "the time will come when men will not put up with sound doctrine" (II Timothy 4:3).[25]

Revelation says over and over that "the Word of God and the testimony of Jesus Christ" (Revelation 1:2,9; 6:9; 20:4) is of the utmost importance. Revelation 12:17 indicates that the dragon [Satan] was enraged — not at those who had subjective experiences but — at those "who keep the commandments of God and hold to the testimony of Jesus."

During my early ministry days, I found myself so absorbed in researching the cults, occult, and New Age that I spent more time reading books and magazines than I did God's Word, and it began to trouble me. So in 1989, after a time of intense prayer and fasting, and extensive Scripture study, I made a commitment to read His Word and pray three times a day. And except for valuable resource material, I gave most of my books away. It has proven to be one of the most beneficial decisions I have ever made. Now instead of saying what this evangelist or minister or prophet says, I know what God's Word says (and more importantly I *know* the Author), and that's my confidence.

The Satanic "Blessing"

I asked a pastor who had been attending various ministers' conferences where they are promoting some blatantly unscriptural teachings and practices, "Why are so many pastors getting involved?" He said, "The Church is hurting and this seems to be where all the excitement and growth is at!" Such pastors conclude that since they have growth and excitement, they are "justified" in forgetting God's Word, accepting an imitation of God's genuine Spirit, and involving themselves in beliefs and practices that will supposedly help their church or ministry grow.

Many ministers and churches are experiencing what I call a "satanic blessing." They're allowing New Age and occult techniques to infiltrate their churches and ministries, and they're seeing excitement. They're seeing what appears to be blessing and growth, popularity and prosperity. They're saying: "It must be from God. There's so much love and unity. Things are going so well!" But I say: "It's a deceptive blessing and is only temporary!"

In contrast, I am seeing many churches proclaiming Biblical Christianity — and they are alive, on fire, filled with the Spirit, and many are growing numerically and in the *true* power and knowledge of the Lord Jesus Christ! God always preserves a faithful remnant.

While Satan pours out his spirit of deception among the Biblical illiterate, God pours out among the faithful remnant a much greater anointing and resurrection power of His Spirit — the Spirit of Truth. And those who are His own and who stay committed and true to His Word and Spirit will walk in greater power, authority, and victory than ever before.

One day the popular, wealthy, and unified apostate church that makes those who dwell on earth drunk with the wine of her spiritual adultery will be destroyed. Revelation 17:16,17 gives us the following account:

> And the ten horns which you saw, and the beast [Antichrist], these will hate the harlot and will make her desolate and naked, and will eat her flesh and will

burn her up with fire. For God has put it in their hearts to execute His purpose by having a common purpose, and by giving their kingdom to the beast, until the words of God should be fulfilled.

In contrast, true believers in Christ — those committed to the testimony of the Jesus of the Bible and obedient to the Word of God — will rule and reign with Christ for all eternity.

The "King Saul Move"

I see many Christians involved in what I call a "King Saul Move." King Saul started out obeying the Lord, and God greatly blessed him, until Saul began to disobey and rebel. When God no longer answered his prayers, King Saul went to the witch of Endor for advice. Instead he should have humbled himself, repented, and sought the Lord with all his heart.

Likewise, many Christians today are unwilling to repent and turn from hidden sins and false teachings and turn back to Biblical Christianity with all their hearts. As a result they no longer hear God's voice and God no longer answers their prayers. They no longer walk in His presence, peace, and power. They become frustrated and discouraged. They think that the Bible doesn't work and the Lord has been unfaithful. They become vulnerable to false teachings and "new revelations" and phenomena that go contrary to the Scriptures. But with each of these people, you can trace it back to decisions they made or involvements that were against God's will and in violation of Biblical principles. Like Saul who went to the witch of Endor, many of these Christians involve themselves in New Age and occult techniques.

Why settle for an inferior, counterfeit technique when you can have the genuine power of God's Spirit? You can walk in God's presence and peace if you seek Him with all your heart. Before the Lord, I call you back to your first love and into pure, unadulterated devotion to Him and His Word!

I don't care how many people tell you to believe

something or how many Christian leaders are involved in this new technique or practice. I don't care how many Christians are jumping on the bandwagon of this "new revelation." If it's not in accord with God's Word, reject it!

I have seen many "spiritual bandwagons" come and go. I have watched many Christians get "blown here and there by every wind of teaching" (Ephesians 4:14 - NIV), but I have chosen to stay firmly grounded on the solid Rock of God's Word.

Belshazzar's Final Fling

Belshazzar, king of Babylon, had a "final fling" in Daniel 5. So too, the apostate church is having her "final fling." While a lost and dying world goes to a Christ-less eternity, an excitement-crazed church "parties in the Spirit" — drunk, laughing, falling over, dancing sensually, involving themselves in New Age and occult techniques, and giving "new revelations" and "prophecies" that only encourage their foolish and errant ways. But the party is about to come to an end. The handwriting is on the wall.

Prophecy is being fulfilled. The New World Order and the deceptive temporary reign of Antichrist and the False Prophet looms on the horizon. Potential persecution and martyrdom for true believers in Christ draw ever closer. Apostasy accelerates, yet few seem to notice or care. The approaching tribulation of Antichrist's reign of terror, God's wrath and judgment, and Christ's Second Coming are ignored or distorted by supposed believers in Christ who are too busy partying and having a "good time in the Lord" to realize the signs of the times that are being fulfilled.

Concerning the end times Daniel 12:10 states:

> Many will be purged, purified and refined; but the wicked will act wickedly, and none of the wicked will understand, but those who have insight will understand.

Belshazzar, who had been drinking wine, was unprepared for the attack of Darius the Mede and was slain by him. So too, a "church" drunk on the "new wine" will also be unprepared for what lies ahead, and will be "slain" with little resistance.

Belshazzar, who had become preoccupied with partying and feeling good, was oblivious to what was about to happen. But Daniel knew, and so will you know of the impending events that are to come in the last days, if you read the Word and get on your knees in prayer like he did. Doing so will help you have the same discernment and ultimate victory Daniel had.

David Wilkerson states it this way:

> The Lord has a people in these confusing times who are not confused. They are so given to Jesus — so in love with Him, so open to the reproof of His Spirit, so separated from the wickedness of this age — that they know the ways and workings of the Holy Spirit. They know what is pure and holy, and what is fleshly and foolish .... [26]

In Daniel chapter 6, Daniel was appointed to leadership in Darius the Mede's new kingdom. Likewise, those who stay true to the Lord and honor His Word, will be the ones whom God will eventually honor and vindicate and empower.

When King Belshazzar offered Daniel great rewards for giving the interpretation of the handwriting on the wall, Daniel answered the king by saying:

> Keep your gifts for yourself, or give your rewards to someone else; however, I will read the inscription to the king and make the interpretation known to him (Daniel 5:17).

I have had numerous opportunities throughout the years to compromise. I have been told that if I would just jump on the bandwagon of the current trends, I could have an even greater ministry. My response is similar to Daniel's:

> Keep your gifts, keep your popularity. All I want is Jesus Christ. All I want is to walk in obedience to His Word. All I want is to walk in sensitivity and submission to the leading of His Spirit.

I don't want anything the *world* has to offer in that regard. I've had my chance to have that, and I've rejected it the way Moses rejected the riches of Egypt!

When I gave my life to Christ, I gave up everything for Him. Why should I now — when we are so close to His return — sell Him out and go the convenient, popular way?

You can have your fleeting fame. You can have your temporary excitement and power. You can get involved in apostasy and enjoy the momentary pleasure of committing spiritual adultery. But there will be a time in the very near future when God's "handwriting" will be manifest and your face will grow pale and your knees will shake like Belshazzar's. Just as no conjurers or diviners could charm Belshazzar's dilemma away, no inner healing, visualization, positive confession, personal prophecy, "new revelation," imitation experience, or counterfeit miracle — not even a unified apostate church bent on world conquest — will be able to deliver you.

More Blatant Forms of Occultism

A man came into our ministry center requesting information on Halloween. From the conversation I discovered that he was in leadership in a church propagating many of the techniques and beliefs I am exposing in this book. I asked, "How can you discern the spirit of occultism in Halloween, but you cannot discern the spirit of occultism that has infiltrated your church?" He had no real answer.

Christians who have become lukewarm and don't know God's Word, lack discernment and are getting involved in New Age and occult beliefs and techniques. They will eventually, if they do not repent, get into more blatant forms of occultism. Unless they repent this very mentality and spirit may one day result in their taking the mark of the beast. This is a strong statement, but it is a response to what I have seen — a gradual but continual undermining of many people's commitment to the Christ of the Bible, and a growing tolerance and encouragement of occultism.

Many years ago I said that we would one day see churches that once loved the Lord committing spiritual adultery by bringing occultism into the church. We are now seeing it. Many have replaced commitment to the Christ of the Bible and obedience to God's Word and the genuine moving of God's Spirit with occultic techniques and beliefs that they have tried to Christianize. We will soon see blatant occultism, sexual immorality, lewd dancing, and other manifestations around the altars of many churches. Many church services will more resemble the revelry around the golden calf in Exodus 32 than a gathering of New Testament Spirit-filled believers. The words written about Aaron in Exodus 32:25 will be true of many pastors:

> Moses saw that the people were running wild and that Aaron had let them get out of control and so become a laughingstock to their enemies (NIV).

You who participate in New Age and occult beliefs and practices must repent. Turn away from them. Return to sound Scriptural beliefs and practices, or drift further and further from the truth.

Those of you who do not repent of these activities may think you are walking with the God of the Bible, but your teachings, practices, and fruit prove otherwise. You might believe you are being led by God's Spirit and operating the gifts of the Holy Spirit, but the fact is you are becoming far removed from Biblical Christianity.

Initially most people thought these new teachings and practices were merely new insights from God's Word. But now that it is becoming more and more occultic in nature, many are realizing the true source and inspiration.

We are seeing the fulfillment of what John in Revelation, and Paul in II Thessalonians, and Jesus in Matthew 24, prophesied. We are on the verge of Christ's Second Coming, yet much of the Church is in spiritual adultery.

We're Called to Purity — Not Adultery

My heart breaks when I see the deception and error in the body of Christ. Many are rising up in Christ's name and seducing His bride into spiritual adultery through false prophecies, pseudo miracles, and occultic phenomena.

I feel like Paul, who said in II Corinthians 11:2-4:

> I am jealous for you with a godly jealousy. I promised you to one husband, to Christ, so that I might present you as a pure virgin to Him. But I am afraid that just as Eve was deceived by the serpent's cunning, your minds may somehow be led astray from your sincere and pure devotion to Christ. For if someone comes to you and preaches a Jesus other than the Jesus we preached, or if you receive a different spirit from the one you received, or a different gospel from the one you accepted, you put up with it easily enough. (NIV)

What is one reason in the New Testament why you can divorce your wife? Adultery. Do you know why in the Old Testament that God temporarily separated Himself from His bride, Israel? It was because of spiritual adultery — unfaithfulness to Him and His Word.

When the Israelites were obedient and followed the Lord with all their hearts, they had blessings and security. But when they were disobedient and followed other gods, they had famines, lost wars, and eventually went into captivity.

He let Israel (the ten northern tribes) go into Assyrian captivity (722 B.C.), and He let Judah be taken into Babylonian captivity (586 B.C.) for one main reason — spiritual adultery.

God created us to have a relationship with Him, to be His bride. When God sees His bride being a prostitute by committing spiritual adultery, it offends and angers Him in the same way it would hurt and anger you if your mate cheated on you.

Hosea says concerning God's people:

> For a spirit of harlotry has led them astray, and they have played the harlot, departing from their God (Hosea 4:12).

In fact the entire book of Hosea deals with Israel's harlotry, God's judgment because of it, and God's forgiveness and restoration. A few other Scriptures which reveal God's displeasure with spiritual adultery are: Leviticus 20:6; Psalm 106:35-40; Jeremiah 3:1-25; Ezekiel 16:1-43; 23:1-49; Revelation 17:1-19:2.

Be Hot or Cold, but Not Lukewarm

In Revelation 3:15-19, the resurrected Christ gives a relevant message for the body of Christ today. He says:

> I know your deeds, that you are neither cold nor hot; I would that you were cold or hot. So because you are lukewarm, and neither hot nor cold, I will spit you out of My mouth. Because you say, "I am rich, and have become wealthy, and have need of nothing," and you do not know that you are wretched and miserable and poor and blind and naked, I advise you to buy from Me gold refined by fire, that you may become rich, and white garments, that you may clothe yourself, and that the shame of your nakedness may not be revealed; and eye salve to anoint your eyes, that you may see. Those whom I love, I reprove and discipline; be zealous therefore, and repent.

God is saying to you today that if you want to compromise and be cold towards Him, then you can have your temporary pleasure. But He would rather you were hot and would serve Him with all your heart. Don't be lukewarm. Don't have that unholy mix of using His name and twisting His Word and then seducing His people into occultism, New Ageism, and spiritual adultery.

Three Woes

It is in searching the Scripture, fasting, and prayer that I hear from the Lord. During such a time the Lord spoke to my heart that one of my main desires and prayers should be: "Lord, use me to turn the hearts of Your people back to You, or let me die trying!" I had it put on a poster and it hangs in my office to this day as a continual reminder.

In Matthew 23, Jesus gave several woes. And in keeping with that theme, I want to list for you three warnings to the body of Christ that the Lord strongly impressed upon my heart and mind on an occasion of being on my knees before Him in prayer and fasting:

1) Woe to you who replace walking in obedience to God's Word, and receiving the genuine transforming power of His Holy Spirit, with psychospiritual

techniques, emotionalism, mind control, occultic techniques, or pseudo miracles!

2) Woe to you who attempt to manipulate God or usurp His Lordship by confessing your own will instead of seeking and submitting to His!

3) Woe to you who prophesy falsely and of your own inspiration, or who seek and follow the word of a "prophet" and "new revelations" more than you seek and follow the Word of God!

Repent and return to Biblical Christianity. Be hot, not lukewarm. For greatly blessed is the one who wholeheartedly follows the Lord!

Return to Your First Love

Return to your first love — the Jesus of the Bible. Return to obedience to His Word and His Spirit. Desire the Lord more than anyone or anything else on earth. Come out from among those who are seducing you into committing spiritual adultery.

I pray you will turn to the Lord with your whole heart. Today the Lord is calling you back by His Spirit to make a commitment to Him, to walk in obedience to His Word, to walk in the true power of His Spirit, and to honor and glorify Him in all things. Do not be a spiritual prostitute, but stay true to the God of the Bible.

Keep on Course With Discernment

I was speaking at a convention in the Himalayas during my first India outreach. We had to walk on mountain trails from where we were staying at the orphanage to get to the convention site. At night it was so dark we had to use flashlights.

The final night of the convention I decided to stay back at the orphanage by myself to spend some extra time in prayer before my last message. When it was time for me to go, I realized it was almost pitch black, with just a little light from the moon and stars. So I walked the mountain trail alone with just a small flashlight. It's amazing how a trail that takes five minutes to walk in the daytime becomes so difficult to walk at night, especially when you're all by yourself.

By then the convention was already going on. They were singing and I was supposed to be the featured speaker, so I prayed, "Lord, it's going to be a little bit of an adventure. You have to help me take the correct path."

I had to do two things to keep myself on course. First, I had to be very sensitive to my environment. I had to shine my flashlight onto my path and watch for trees, rocks, a narrow wooden bridge over a mountain stream, and other sign posts I could recognize, to make certain I was going the right way. I also had to feel with my feet so I did not fall over any of the many rocks scattered along the way.

Secondly, I had to be very sensitive to listen to the singing to make certain the path I was taking was getting me closer and closer to the convention site. I also had to be sensitive to hear the sound of running water, so I would know I was going over the right mountain stream.

Many trails in the mountains intersect each other. It was imperative that I take the correct trail, not only so I could make it to the convention, but also because one wrong turn could cause me to be lost in the Himalayas all night, and possibly freeze to death.

So too, today there are many "intersecting" spiritual teachings, techniques, and experiences. We, therefore, must know the "environment" of God's Word and must have a sensitivity to and discernment from God's Spirit.

I had to recognize the trees and bridges, and feel around the paths with my feet for rocks, and shine my flashlight on the trail to get to the right location (because to go in the wrong direction could be disastrous). We must know God's Word which "is a lamp to my feet, and a light to my path" (Psalm 119:105), so that we will follow the right path lest we end up in spiritual chaos.

In the same way I had to listen for the running water and listen for the singing, we have to be tuned-in and sensitive to God's Spirit — not to our own inspiration, not to things we want to interpret as being God's Spirit, and not to a counterfeit voice. That only comes by getting into His Word, getting on our knees in prayer and fasting, and by seeking His will with all our hearts. That is what God is calling the body of Christ to do today!

Joshua's Challenge to Only Serve the Lord

After Joshua reviewed many of the great things the Lord had done for the people (Joshua 24:1-13), he challenged them to:

> ... fear the Lord and serve Him in sincerity and truth; and put away the gods which your fathers served beyond the River and in Egypt, and serve the Lord. And if it is disagreeable in your sight to serve the Lord, choose for yourselves today whom you will serve: whether the gods which your fathers served which were beyond the River, or the gods of the Amorites in whose land you are living; but as for me and my house, we will serve the Lord (Joshua 24:14,15).

It was a time for Joshua and the people of Israel to reflect on where they had been, and how God had delivered and preserved them through the trials of the wilderness and the lands of hostile foreign peoples. They recalled how the Lord drove out all their enemies from the land before them. Joshua reminded the Hebrews, however, of God's holiness; that He is a jealous God who will not put up with spiritual adultery.

He declared:

> If you forsake the Lord and serve foreign gods, then He will turn and do you harm and consume you after He has done good to you (Joshua 24:20).

The people committed to Joshua that they would serve the Lord" (Joshua 24:21). Joshua then challenged them to therefore "put away the foreign gods which are in your midst, and incline your hearts to the Lord, the God of Israel" (Joshua 24:23). That very day Joshua made a covenant with the people concerning their commitment to only serve the Lord (Joshua 24:24-27). Further instruction on this matter comes to us from the book of Samuel:

> And Samuel said to the whole house of Israel, "If you are returning to the Lord with all your hearts, then rid

yourselves of the foreign gods and the Ashtoreths and commit yourselves to the Lord and serve Him only ... " (I Samuel 7:3 - NIV).

Take the TV Challenge!

I have challenged many pastors and believers in Christ to turn off their TV for one month. I tell them, "Don't watch any TV or videos, or listen to Christian cassettes, or read Christian books, or attend any Christian seminars or conferences. Instead of getting filtered Scriptural teaching, for just one month read only the Word of God and spend time in prayer and fasting."

Those who have taken the challenge have frequently informed me that this process has helped them see that many of the current teachings, techniques, and phenomena are not Scriptural, and as a result they make a renewed commitment to Biblical Christianity.

When I started into the ministry, I learned that I was not to emulate the great evangelists, or popular preachers, or even my favorite missionaries. Instead of trying to become like them, God showed me that I was to build my life and the work He had called me to on Biblical Christianity. So I turned to the Scriptures, and as I did, I prayed: "Lord, show me what characteristics and qualities You require of those who are to serve You. What do YOU want?" He showed me in the lives of the heroes of the faith. It was by examining their lives that I learned those things that are pleasing to God and those things He finds repulsive. As I read His Word, I saw firsthand how God dealt with Noah, Abraham, Joseph, Moses, David, and other leaders; how He spoke through His prophets who proclaimed, "Thus saith the Lord;" and how in Romans 8:29, He desires for me and all Christians to ultimately be conformed to the image of His Son, Jesus Christ.

Throughout my ministry I have prayed, "Lord, don't let me attempt to manipulate You into what I want You to be, or what people say You are or think You should be, but reveal Yourself to me as You are. I want to know YOU. I desire that You show me who You are by Your Word and by Your Spirit, then cause me to submit and be conformed to who You are and what You require of me. Enable me to stand for the things You stand for and oppose the things You oppose. Teach me to love the things You love and hate the things You hate."

Those of you who know me, realize that I have been transformed. I have gone from a rebellious, self-seeking youth, to a man who desires more than anything else in the world to know and please the Lord. The only explanation for this transformed and obedient life is that God changed me through hearing His Word and the power of His Holy Spirit. Had I not spent time in prayer and fasting, in reading His Word and applying His principles, I know beyond a shadow of a doubt that my life would have remained unchanged.

I challenge you now to turn off the TV, the videos, the tapes, and for one month read only the Bible in your pursuit of knowing God and His Truth. Your life will be greatly impacted as you put into practice, by the help of His Spirit, the principles He teaches you in His Word. That is what Biblical Christianity is all about, and that is the focus of this ministry. I have tried to build my life and this ministry completely on Biblical principles and the leading of His Spirit. I challenge you to do the same. The rewards are far greater than you can imagine, and far superior to any new revelation, teaching, technique, or phenomena that are currently sweeping the Church.

One benefit is that as you grow in wisdom, you will be able to discern what is truly from God and what is not. As you apply His Truth to your life, you will walk in greater peace, power, and victory than you ever dreamed possible. The Bible calls us to grow in grace, but how can we grow if we don't discipline ourselves to seek the Truth on our own, without being lured by every wind of false doctrine that comes along? Remember, there is a way that seems right to a man, but it leads to destruction. You must turn aside from that way. It is the broad way. But how will you know that unless you delve into Scripture and hide it in your heart? Biblical Christianity begins with:

• knowing the Word (Christ is the Word, John 1);

- knowing the God who inspired that Word;
- and by being empowered by His Holy Spirit.

When these three aspects of the Christian life are operative in you, you are enabled to be a bold witness for His Truth and to discern deception.

Do you want to be a Biblical Christian and know if today's trends and phenomena are of God or not? Then take my challenge:

For one month turn off your TV, choose neither to listen to any teaching tapes or videos nor to read books other than the Bible, and avoid seminars or conferences. Spend some of the time fasting and seeking God on your knees in prayer. Ask Him to make His Word known to you and its meaning clear by His Spirit. Temporarily put aside the teachings of your favorite TV evangelist or renowned radio preacher, and instead wait upon the Lord. Hear the Word of the Lord as you pour over the Scriptures. Meditate and reflect on what you are reading, and listen as God instructs you.

I have yet to see anyone who has genuinely and earnestly done this return to me afterward without having a whole new perspective on life. They see in a new light today's erroneous trends and heresies that are infiltrating Christ's Church, and are well on their way to living a Biblical Christian life.

When You Know the Genuine — You'll Spot the Counterfeit

By the time you finish reading this book, no doubt there will be more false teachings, fads, phenomena, and trends that will sweep the church — most likely "old" heresies in modern garb. Jesus gave a parable about a man who sowed good seed in his field, only to discover an enemy sowed tares among the wheat. The tares did not become evident until the wheat sprouted and bore grain. When asked if he wanted his servants to gather up the tares, the man told them to "allow both to grow together until the harvest" (Matthew 13:30). During the explanation of the parable to His disciples Jesus stated:

Therefore just as the tares are gathered up and burned with fire, so shall it be at the end of the age. The Son of Man will send forth His angels, and they will gather out of His kingdom all stumbling blocks, and those who commit lawlessness, and will cast them into the furnace of fire; in that place there shall be weeping and gnashing of teeth. Then the righteous will shine forth as the sun in the kingdom of their Father. He who has ears, let him hear (Matthew 13:40-43).

We are called to expose error and to contend for the faith even though false teachers and teachings will continue until the Lord returns. Yes, it is difficult to try to keep up with every wind of false doctrine. It is necessary to safeguard your mind from these false teachings by properly studying the Word, and by prayerfully developing an ongoing relationship with the Lord through the power of His Holy Spirit. This is absolutely necessary in order to guard yourself against the subtle error that so easily captures the hearts and minds of the unsuspecting.

Don't be worried about identifying each deception that comes along; rather, get to know the genuine by studying the Word of God, and the rest will take care of itself. Then you will be able to identify the imitation and the counterfeit and lead others to a knowledge of the Truth.

So get to know the authentic, and you will have developed a healthy spirit of discernment which will guard your mind and your heart against the corrupt teachings of those who are "deceiving and being deceived" (II Timothy 3:13).

As a watchman, I have sounded the alarm and I have warned the body of Christ. I have obeyed what Scripture instructs and what the Holy Spirit has led me to do. The choice is now yours.

My closing words to you are those of Paul to the Corinthians: "Be on your guard; stand firm in the faith; be men of courage; be strong. Do everything in love" (I Corinthians 16:13,14 NIV).

Endnotes

1   Interview by Russell Chandler, *Paul McGuire: Escaping the New Age, Charisma & Christian Life,* Strang Communications Co., May 1989, p. 65.

2   Johanna Michaelsen, *Like Lambs to the Slaughter,* Harvest House Publishers, Eugene, OR, 1989, p. 123.

3   Napoleon Hill, *Think and Grow Rich,* Random House, pp. 213, 214, 215, 217, 218.

4   Martin L. Rossman, M.D., *The Healing Power of Imagery, New Age Journal,* March/April 1988, pp. 53-56.

5   Kurt Koch, *Occult ABC,* Kregel Publications, Grand Rapids, MI, 1978, p. 95.

6   Wilson & Weldon, *Occult Shock,* Master Books, San Diego, CA, 1980, pp. 227, 228.

7   Peter & Patti Lalonde, eds., *Omega Letter,* Ontario, Canada, vol. 2:10, Nov. 1987.

8   Lawrence O. Richards, *Expository Dictionary of Bible Words,* Zondervan Publishing House, Grand Rapids, MI, 1985, pp. 505, 507.

9   Donald Gee, *Concerning Spiritual Gifts,* Gospel Publishing House, Springfield, MO, pp. 43, 44.

10 *People & Events, Charisma & Christian Life,* Feb. 1990, p. 16.

11 Donald C. Stamps, ed., *The Full Life Study Bible,* Zondervan Publishing House, Grand Rapids, MI, "Introduction: Jeremiah," 1992, p. 1079.

12 Bill Rudge, *A Cult & 'Extreme Group' Awareness Alphabet,* Bill Rudge Ministries, Hermitage, PA, 1982, pp. 24, 25.

13 *The Full Life Study Bible,* from I Corinthians 14:24 footnote, p. 1775.

14 W. Phillip Keller, *Predators In Our Pulpits,* Harvest House Publishers, Eugene, OR, 1988, pp. 77, 78.

15 David Wilkerson, *Times Square Church Pulpit Series,* Sept. 1995.

Endnotes

16 David A. Sabella — Taken from preliminary Greek exegesis research developed for the paper: *An Exegetical Study of Ephesians 5:19 and Colossians 3:16*, for M.Div. requirement at RPT Seminary, May, 1995.

17 George A. Buttrick, ed., *The Interpreter's Bible*, Volume X, Abingdon Press, Nashville, TN, 1953, p. 714.

18 Excerpted from:

Rabindranath R. Maharaj (with Dave Hunt), Death of A Guru, A. J. Holman Company, Philadelphia, PA, 1977.

Tal Brooke (research by John Weldon), *Riders of the Cosmic Circuit*, Lion Publishing, England, 1986.

19 *Spiritual Counterfeits Project Newsletter*, Volume 19:4, SCP, Inc., Spring 1995, p. 8.

20-23

Spiritual Counterfeits Project Newsletter, Volume 19:2, Fall 1994, p. 14.

24 Johanna Michaelsen, *The Beautiful Side of Evil*, Harvest House Publishers, Eugene, OR, 1982, pp. 179, 183, 184.

25 George O. Wood, Unpublished Article: *The Laughing Revival*, Springfield, MO, 1995.

26 David Wilkerson, *Times Square Church Pulpit Series*, Sept. 1995.

FOR MORE INFORMATION:

Bill Rudge has produced numerous books, pamphlets, and cassettes on a variety of other timely topics. For a complete listing and a copy of his informative newsletter, write to:

Bill Rudge Ministries
P.O. Box 108
Sharon, PA 16146-0108